Walking
the Llano

Walking *the* *Llano*

A TEXAS MEMOIR OF PLACE

Shelley Armitage

UNIVERSITY OF OKLAHOMA PRESS : NORMAN

Also by Shelley Armitage

(co-editor) *Reading into Photography: Selected Essays, 1959–1980* (Albuquerque, 1982)
John Held, Jr., Illustrator of the Jazz Age (Syracuse, N.Y., 1987)
(editor) *Wind's Trail: The Early Life of Mary Austin* (Santa Fe, 1990)
Peggy Pond Church (Boise, Idaho, 1993)
Kewpies and Beyond: The World of Rose O'Neill (Jackson, Miss., 1994)
Women's Work: Essays in Cultural Studies (West Cornwall, Conn., 1995)
Bones Incandescent: The Pajarito Journals of Peggy Pond Church (Lubbock, Tex., 2001)

This book is published with the generous assistance of
The McCasland Foundation, Duncan, Oklahoma.

Portions of this book previously appeared in Shelley Armitage, "Prairie Interrupted," in
To Everything on Earth: New Writing on Fate, Community, and Nature, © 2010 by Kurt
Caswell, Susan Tomlinson, and Diane Warner, published by Texas Tech University Press,
and in Shelley Armitage, "Writing Llano," in *Writing on the Wind: An Anthology of West
Texas Women Writers,* © 2005 by Texas Tech University Press. Reprinted by permission
of Texas Tech University Press.

Library of Congress Cataloging-in-Publication Data

Armitage, Shelley, 1947–
Walking the Llano : a Texas memoir of place / Shelley Armitage.
pages cm
ISBN 978-0-8061-5162-5 (hardcover : alkaline paper)
1. Armitage, Shelley, 1947– 2. Vega (Tex.)—Biography. 3. Vega (Tex.)—History.
4. Oldham County (Tex.)—History. 5. Llano Estacado—History.
6. Llano Estacado—Description and travel. 7. Place attachment—Llano Estacado.
8. Vega (Tex.)—Environmental conditions. 9. Oldham County (Tex.)—Environmental
conditions. 10. Llano Estacado—Environmental conditions. I. Title.
F394.V5A76 2016
976.4'824063092—dc23
[B]
2015025692

The paper in this book meets the guidelines for permanence and durability of the
Committee on Production Guidelines for Book Longevity of the Council on Library
Resources, Inc. ∞

1 2 3 4 5 6 7 8 9 10

For my loving parents,
Dorothy Mae Armitage and Bob Armitage,
and in memory of my brother, Roy,
adventurers and stewards all.
And for the land: may your amazing blessings survive us.

Contents

Illustrations

Walking
the Llano

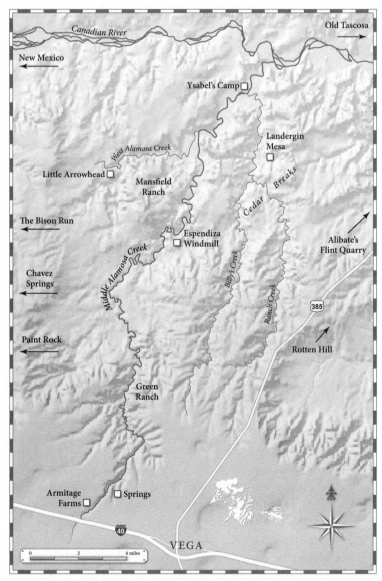

Map of the Middle Alamosa Creek. *Map by Gerry Krieg.*

Introduction

Writing Llano

Ψ *[T]he term landscape, as it has entered the English language, is misleading. "A portion of territory the eye can comprehend in a single view" does not correctly describe the relationship between the human being and his or her surroundings. This assumes the viewer is somehow outside or separate from the territory he or she surveys. Viewers are as much a part of the landscape as the boulders they stand on.*—LESLIE MARMON SILKO

Ψ *Why is there no poet of the plains?*—MAY SARTON

This was the second time the sheriff's deputy had been to my house—and this time he had a shotgun. "He doesn't remember," I said to myself, noting his glancing look, polite but without recognition. Then again, was it embarrassment? The first time he came it was midnight, a cold, black winter night when I had returned to Vega from El Paso for the weekend but somehow arrived without my house keys. I immediately went to the sheriff's office, where I hoped the dispatcher would produce keys to my house (as a courtesy in this small town, you could leave copies there; I had left some years ago). She looked me over, cool but assessing, when I entered the building. After all, she was there alone, too. We rummaged through the pile as she explained that old sets had been culled and removed. No keys.

She called the deputy, who was cruising somewhere around town—the mile-square rural community located almost at the midway point of old Route 66, population 952. The main concern of law enforcement here was drug transportation along Interstate 40. They

3

hardly ever checked my neighborhood. With only three houses—two belonging to ranch families and one to an eighty-year-old widow on my street—and my house at the dead end, it was not the most compelling beat.

The deputy met me at my house. I had already managed to get in through the back door with a separate set of keys recovered from a coffee can in my garden bed. But the interior door was locked from inside, and the only possibility of entry was through the small beveled windows up top. I persuaded him to try to get his hand through a window by climbing up on some boxes on the back porch, precarious because they tended to give with too much weight. I found myself holding on to one of his legs as he shimmied up—and after several protests and my insistence—he busted the pane, broke into my house, reached inside, and unlocked the door.

Now it was time for *me* to be embarrassed, as I remembered the bizarre circumstances that evening and my pressuring him to break the law so that I could hastily get to the bathroom and sleep in my own bed. Immediately regretting the loss of the beveled glass, irreplaceable as one of the period appointments of the hand-built 1920s bungalow, I would lamely cover the broken pane with cut cardboard that whistled and slipped loose when any wind pressure sifted through the house.

You'd think I would've learned not to make another hasty decision, but now I said, "Guess we've got to shoot him, huh?"

He shifted his gun to what I could tell was his shooting shoulder. "Yeah, not much else you can do."

I went again through the possible options. Trap him, move him, anything else at all? I had inquired around about alternatives. I lived outside the city limits so there was no Animal Control to call. Trapping a porcupine was difficult. They don't have a good sense of smell. And just stunning one is problematic, particularly this one, nestled comfortably in the bough of my largest, oldest elm.

"Can't afford to lose the tree," I said, reiterating my concerns. Healthy elms are prizes in prairie country. Porcupines can strip the bark from them in no time, weakening and eventually killing the tree. This one, about eighty feet high, shaded the south side of the house. Dead, it would be hard to remove.

Robert "Bob" Armitage at the farm. *Author photo.*

The list of justifications for shooting a living creature in my yard came to a halt when the shot went off and the porcupine fell like a stone, heavy and quick. The gloved deputy picked him up, commented that he was young. Close up, his quills looked soft.

Only then did I notice the feet, the black-padded bottoms, pattycake-like, shaped like a human baby's—tiny feet, the kind pressed into a mold to remember. Instantly I felt kin and more than deep regret. Had I killed a part of myself? Up in the tree, he had looked so different. Yes, napping and benign, but a mere dark hump on the trunk, distant enough to be objectified, deemed varmint. The deputy swung him into the back of the pickup; I wanted to turn my eyes away.

Life on a prairie, lived close, involves these kinds of choices, lapsed realizations. My dad had been what was called in the 1930s a "suitcase farmer," someone who doesn't live on his farm. We lived in town. The farm was three miles northwest of town, divided into two sections: the South Place bordering Interstate 40, the North Place five miles out, bordering the Canadian River breaks. But for as long as I can remember, my dad went to the farm every day, often twice. It was like a family member, something to be cared for, cherished. The

Methodist sermons on Stewardship Sunday resonated, even as Daddy sat stiffly, perhaps napping, at the end of the pew. I thought of my dad as a steward: he took care of the land.

"Care" meant making difficult decisions, like shooting a cow left paralyzed and hopeless after a breach birth. It meant aerial spray to exterminate pests and kill the bindweed that choked the crops, despite the dangers to other living things. It also meant watching, tending, repairing, and focusing on a future beyond immediate gain. There were the cattle to be fed during snowstorms, the sickly calves brought into town, sheltered and nursed in the barn.

When I rode to the farm with my dad and granddad as a girl, the men plotted breeding and crop rotation possibilities, smoking their cigarettes, the windows all down, I sat in the back and cried because the grasshoppers flew through the windows and onto my clothes, into my hair, sometimes into my mouth. I was told to stop that crying or I couldn't come to the farm anymore, and *if you'll stop that crying, keep your mouth closed, the grasshoppers will stay out too.*

Plowing, my brother turned up a family of cottontails. When my parents got home from work, they found six small bunnies skittering around in the clawfoot bathtub. They were compensation, as my brother knew, for the recent loss of our pet rabbits. We'd discovered eight grisly heads suspended in their cages, the bodies ripped through the cage slats by a pack of dogs. Another bad decision, those elevated, slat-floored cages? The image haunted me, a permanent clutch in my stomach.

I've always said of my Vega house that I lived in the middle of a prairie, and try as I might to have a "yard," it was still a prairie. My parents' yard there had trees, a small rose garden. But their house fronted a large pasture in which, as a kid, I coursed up and down, looking for surprises. My Vega bungalow is surrounded by an acre on each of three sides, with a fifty-acre pasture in front. Originally, it had been part of a small farm. And my "yard" remains prairie, mostly native grass (which I do encourage), forbs, weeds, an occasional rattlesnake, more frequently bull snakes, and sometimes a porcupine.

A prairie puts you close to all its animal occupants, both wild and domestic. One summer in my Vega farmhouse, I was cleaning, enjoying the fresh air through the screen door, playing jazz music on the record player. I heard something on the porch, a scratching sound, and went to see. It was what looked like a banty rooster—cocked head, perky walk, curious. He stayed around, disappeared, then showed up when I played music again the next day. And the next. It became a joke—the Jazz Chicken, I called him. He began to roost on the porch at night, on an old table by the door. When I would come in late from dates (well, late to *him*), he'd cock his head and open one eye as if I had violated curfew. This comic relationship continued until one day he was gone. Upset and fearful, I searched until I found a pile of feathers at the side of the house. Apparently, a skunk had gotten him, or maybe a cat. Only his tiny yellow legs and the feathers remained. At least that is what I thought until my boyfriend, Bill, offered to bury him. "He's a she," Bill said, handing me a tiny banty egg. In the life and death struggle, somehow an unbroken egg survived.

Then there were Pal and Honey, black and golden cocker spaniels belonging to my brother and me. When our cat Ditty (as a kid I couldn't say "kitty") was shot at by some BB-gun-toting boys and ran off, abandoning her four kittens, Honey, who had just had puppies, nursed both. The kitties and puppies nuzzled Honey together as Pal looked on. Honey later died from a rattlesnake bite on her muzzle, but Pal lived to old age until the developing state highway in front of my parents' house provided one car chase too many.

If there weren't animals around, there were stories of them. Almost every time I slept over at my grandparents,' my grandmother put me to sleep by telling some story of their lives in Arkansas in 1909, when "Dad," my grandfather, worked for the early-day U.S. Forest Service in the mountains around Mena. There was the story of the pet squirrel who filled Dad's boots with nuts every night after he went to bed. Dad emptied his boots on the steps from the upstairs bedroom as his morning ritual. Then there was the fox, also a pet, who carried off not only food but also Dad's boots and hid them. This was the fox who animated my dreams. Mom said I would jump up in the middle of the night and leap to the other end of the bed, like a dog that moans and churns its feet during dreams. I prize a photograph of my granddad, decked out in sheepskin chaps and towering

R. W. Armitage (*left*) at Cold Mountain Ranger Station, Mena,
Arkansas. *Author photo.*

Stetson standing next to his saddle horse at the Cold Water Ranger
Station in the early days of the forest service, in Mena. With each of
the bearded men's horses loaded with rifles and serious bedrolls and
camping gear, you might think they were a gang of rustlers or surly
mountain men.

I think that photograph of my granddad was my first image of a
western man.

Certainly I'd thought of my dad, all six-foot-three, James Arness–
looking feet of him, as embodying a masculinity linked to the
outdoors, firm but gentle. Like all western men, my dad wore cowboy

Bob Armitage near the South Draw, Armitage Farms, 1929.
Author photo.

hats and, later in life, seed caps with the logo of some local company
on the front. But I knew my dad as a bald-headed man, someone
who joked about it: "I'm going to comb my hair . . . Both of them," he
would say. When I was a child, my mother showed me photographs
of my dad at their wedding; he had hair and I exclaimed: "That's not
my daddy!" Then she showed me an even earlier photo that further
stretched credulity. What looked to be a boy, arms akimbo, dress
slacks, shirt, hat, and buoyant tie (caught in the Panhandle wind),
stood amidst those prairie grasses, buffalo, side oats grama, and
sacaton, with a wheat stalk in his mouth. The horizon line stretched

behind him, heart high. Now I know this photograph to be exactly my daddy. It was taken when he first began buying the farm as a young teller at the First State Bank in Vega. In photographic terms, he occupies the middle ground between the foreground and background. In prairie terms, the landscape line runs through him.

⋎ Our prairies are severely altered, nothing like the short-grass prairie reported by the earliest chroniclers, the Spanish. Human occupation necessarily means fragmentation, habitat loss. In Oldham County, where Vega is the county seat, sheep, cattle, farming, strip mining, oil, gas exploration, feed lots, dairies, microwave and cell phone towers, and now wind turbines have permanently changed that "sea of grass" early explorers deemed uninhabitable. One of the oldest recorded sites, locally called Milkweed, a sizeable playa lake north of Vega that helped sustain American Indian, Spanish, and early pioneering trails between the Midwest and California, until recently functioned also as a wetlands, attracting blue herons and a variety of ducks and shore birds. The early-day cowboys from the LS, LIT, and XIT ranches horsed around and bathed there. Recently, the city of Vega, pleading issues of flooding in town, cut off the natural drainage to the playa. Now it is dry.

But a lived prairie, even if visited, even if altered, teems.

The Vega community sits atop the northern fringe of the Llano Estacado at an elevation of four thousand feet. The *llano* is part of one of the largest plateaus in North America, stretching from our area west beyond Adrian, Texas, into eastern New Mexico, to the east near the Oklahoma border, then south to the Edwards Plateau near Midland, Texas—32,000 square miles. Authorities differ on the origin of its name, but most agree that "Staked Plains" references the palisade-like formations that, particularly from the west, suggest stakes or stockades. Rising to five thousand feet northwest of Vega, these palisades support the "featureless" prairie, giving credibility to a further speculation that "stakes" might have been used by early travelers to mark the way. Despite the exceedingly rapid growth of the area in the 1930s due to the discovery and development of oil and gas fields—the 1880s population of 387 reaching 1,500 in 1932—the Canadian River valley twelve miles north remains largely the territory

Llano grasslands. *Author photo.*

of pronghorns and deer, artifacts signaling early occupants, and of course cattle. So the overwhelming context of our local grasslands is this southern end of the Great Plains, *this llano.*

Since the 1880s, Oldham County has grown by only two thousand residents. Privately owned ranches, not public lands or small farms, comprise the area north of Vega in Oldham County, nearly two-thirds of the county's 1,501 square miles, including the Canadian Breaks—draws, arroyos, canyons, tributaries—which break up the llano as the land tips toward the Canadian River, dropping in elevation some six hundred feet. The river, 906 miles long, heading a mile north of the New Mexico line in Animas County, Colorado, and crossing the Texas Panhandle into Oklahoma, is a tributary of the Arkansas, joining that river six miles west of the Arkansas line in Oklahoma.

Tectonic activity of the Rocky Mountains and subsequent disbursal of Pleistocene waters and rock resulted in sandy, clay, and caliche soils, the latter of which forms a solid caprock upon which the llano sits. Captured below and exploited above since the breaking out of the prairie into farms and towns in the early twentieth century is the Ogallala Aquifer, one of the largest in the world.

Armitage Farms is a tiny parenthesis within these vast and persistent prairielands. Its southern mixed farmland and native pastures border Interstate 40, originally Route 66. And its north two hundred acres sit on the edge of the Canadian Breaks. From 1929 to 2012, it was mixed farmland and pasture. Now, utilizing the Conservation Reserve Program, I've put it all back to grass. The usual rebreaking out of the prairie—the plowing and planting that regularly destroyed nesting sites of birds like the threatened nighthawks—was now the first step in restoring habitat. The CRP is at heart a conservation program. At the farm I watched one of my high school friends, Mike Jackson, drill the expensive grass mixes into the previous year's wheat stubble with his fancy rig, one positive improvement of agribusiness in the pursuit of what Wendell Berry calls "agri-culture," a more sustainable and natural relationship of humans with land. What the land had given us—this native prairie with its varieties of forbs and grasses—in small measure was given back, even if many of the program's participants were in it for government payments. I had witnessed the decline of the darting nighthawks, the golden-throated meadowlarks. Now I could look forward to slipping through the fence into the field, like I had as a child in the back pasture, looking for nests and nubile grasses.

⩔ Walking these plains, here on the family farm three miles northwest of Vega in the Texas Panhandle, I lean into a north wind. It's winter, a brown-scape tinged in ochre, dried buffalo and grama grasses, a touch of green in the wintered-over yucca and bear grass. Many of the native prairie grasses, like buffalo grass, retain their nourishment through winter, sustenance hidden in their dun middens. The side oats grama wave like sailboat flags, their tiered semaphores flexed in the wind. Sacaton is stately by comparison, its undulating trunk bearing a sparkler-shaped burst of seeds. Buffalo hugs the ground, short-legged like its namesake. All are fragile at the picking, but moored in the ceaseless prairie wind. This early morning, the sky is a washed blue, except for the horizon line, which is indigo, deeper key to the continual changes in the weather. Here you see "blue northers" building; fronts, snows roll in from the north / northwest. I've ridden this road with my dad since I was a baby, later jogging it, giving the gloved wave back to his one-finger greeting as we passed each other when he drove south back into town. Lately, the resident Swainson's hawk, territorial on his cedar post in early winter, eyes my walk. Running days over, I am slowed to a pace fit for my desire to write the llano, for, pointed north and alone, I understand the act of walking to be writing, the act of writing, listening—inside and out.

What does the land say to us? I've wondered for years. True, there's been no poet of these plains. Plains history is a history of migration, movement, and change—conditions that make people look ahead, look past. Historically these conditions haven't encouraged people to stay long enough to write more than reports, journals, perhaps letters. But there is a poetry of the plains. This part of the llano, both rolling plains and flatlands, exists as a shape of time, requiring the rhythm of a habit of landscape, of the repetition of experiencing. On the family place, the two sections of it, 1,280 acres, I walk the two draws, the rolling breaks in the bordering level ground. These grass-covered cleavages are wind and water courses feeding the intermittent tributary, the Middle Alamosa Creek, which empties into the Canadian River a meandering thirty miles north. In the distance, the faded winter tan and green, the whitened blue of sky tell of slopes and breaks; a slip of silver suggests a playa lake, holder of water. The playas number almost six hundred in the southern llano south of here, shining like silver dollars across the way.

There have been histories: narratives of the American Indians, of the cattle kingdom, of the coming of railroads and the rise of booster towns as the prairie was broken out in the early twentieth century. Mostly, these are a march of dates, a sequential seeing of how a country was eventually "tamed," developed. I think: if we could read the land as poem, we might more intimately learn from it, understand what it says of natural and human cycles—and that sometimes uneasy relationship between them. All the old settlers of this part of the country are gone now, like my dad who came here with his family in 1926 after the flooding of the White, Buffalo, and Mississippi Rivers in Arkansas washed the Armitages from their delta farm. Memories and stories are lost with this group. But lyric, as fragment, reshapes itself through the subsequent generations; what is left goes on. Residual sites, material survivals—landforms, archaeo-logical sites, abandoned *pastores* settlements—require this other way of telling: the llano's.

The imagist poets, particularly those who frequented the New Mexico landscape of Santa Fe and Taos in the 1920 and 1930s, under-stood this other way of knowing—and of telling. Poets such as Alice Corbin Henderson and Harriet Monroe took the land and its peoples as subjects but believed the concrete resonated beyond its descriptive surface. They translated Ezra Pound's ideas about "imagist poetry" to the land's story: an image could supply an instant intuition, catch-ing a motion that generated an intellectual and emotional complex beneath the conventional meaning. The Southwest poet Peggy Pond Church attempted to write poetry whose imagistic aspects functioned as "a tongue for the wilderness." Likewise, Mary Austin said, "It's the land that wants to be said," cautioning that one must possess "a noticing eye" in order to speak for the land. No wonder that later native writers of the llano, such as Rudolfo Anaya and Fabiola Cabeza de Vaca, would find full and cacophonous what early travelers described as a silent, empty land.

The land's own memories, its shaping cycles, including the human occupations, surface only for the observant, who may hear and articulate something of the image and its instant intuitions. Here on our place, up on the high ground on either side of the south to north draws, I find an occasional pottery shard, refugee of some former dwelling. In her journals, Church remarked upon a similar discovery in a cave: an Anasazi shard bearing the fingerprint of its maker. Marveling at the beauty that emerged from such a hard life in an arid land, Church's find prompted an emotional connection: "I remembered how cold such a cave in winter can be." The shards I find so far have no surviving fingerprints, nor do they accomplish the decorative designs and evocative slips of their Pueblo neighbors. Yet the mica-flecked remnants are corrugated, suggesting their maker's desire for beauty in a world of necessity. Once I picked up a pointed, pale white stone, attracted to its unusual shape and color amid the red clay soils. I discovered it was a "scribe"—a stone tool used to "write upon" pottery, pipes, tools. *To make, to mark*. I keep it on my writing desk, sometimes taking it up, poised.

Alice Walker writes about the value of such material objects as an alternative language that speaks of women's peculiar domestic creativity. Such alternative languages—for example, women's gardens and quilt-making—speak to a wisdom passed from generation to generation through various creative acts. These are the kinds of records, another kind of text, that Walker finds unique as women's materialized lyrics of place.

In the Panhandle, few records of women's lives and work survive except in the land's own records. West of our place about twenty miles, in one of the creek beds that served as connecting trails east and west across the llano, there's a curving sandstone ledge banking a mostly dry creek. Underneath this ledge are numerous pictographs, purportedly painted at various times, perhaps earlier than the 1500s but definitely connected to the Comanchero trade between Mexican traders and Pueblo, Comanche, and other Plains Indians. Just east of this location, we kids played archaeologists on a ranch where the sandstone flatlands border the Piedras de Aqua creek and sites of prehistoric and historic settlement. Near circular grinding holes and smoothly worn buffalo trails in the sandstone, we took spoons and forks to the earth, trying to dish up some latent burial ground or shards or something "Indian" to fulfill our imaginations. But the pictographs overlooking the creek were the real treasure. Later, as an adult, I walked there propelled by the same childhood curiosity. Following the lip of the pale gray sandstone along the creek bed, I slipped under the massive overhang on the south side, sheltering the pictographs. The array, recorded in faint blue, red, and ochre, I imagined was a result of women gathering plants for the paints nearby. And here, in another subtle hint of women's presence, I saw a pictograph of what looks to be a Hopi girl, her hair in whorls over her ears, indicating a marriageable age. She appeared alongside the larger, more noted image of Awanyu—the water serpent, but she speaks of women as central to this gathering place.

This image was pleasantly surprising because mostly this area is known as cowboy country. Large ranches dominate the county, and historically the largest ranch in Texas—the XIT, named for the top ten counties in Texas it encompassed—still captures the imagination. But there were cowgirls, too. I remember the Binford ranch women:

Katherine, the mother, and the two daughters, Nan and Barbara. Katherine came with her husband to the area in the 1920s; the couple got off the train where the tracks ended near present-day Wildorado, making the remainder of the way to their homestead by wagon. Adding to their land through the years, the Binfords became a prominent ranching family, with Nan returning from college after her father's death to help her mother run the ranch. The ranch became home to some of the original cowgirls and ranch women who competed in the All-Girl Rodeos. Nan built part of her reputation as a prize-winning cutting horse performer, following her mother's success. Katherine's first competition was among an all-male field of participants in Madison Square Garden, where she was the first woman to compete against men before the circuits were split.

But I remember the Binford women as working ranch women. Nan and her partner of the time, Lonnie, would pull into town with their horse trailer, driving right through the drive-in window of the bank where my parents worked. I tried to imagine the lives of these women in spurs and chaps—a hard life, but one I romanticized as "free," out among the animals, the dawns, the llano.

My mother was no cowgirl. She grew up in McKinney, Texas—east Texas—and moved to Amarillo when she was a girl. The wildest-west story she ever told involved her older brothers, who, learning she had been given a nickel to get a hamburger, promised to take her with them to "an event" if she would share her hamburger. Wanting to be included in her brothers' adventures, she went along and found herself at what was the last hanging in Collins County. The spectacle attracted at least one hundred curious people; the accused claimed to be innocent of the circumstantial evidence used to rule his fate. Only six years old, Mother didn't peer, like her brothers, around the clustered adults. Shocked and horrified, she hid her face. Afterward, her brothers chimed: "Now let's go get that hamburger."

Mother would pet horses, but never ride them; she never rode with my brother Roy, Dad, and me through our legacy of horses. But her loss was even more evident when the yearly Oldham County parade rolled round after one of our dear elderly friends, Carrie, died. Carrie and her husband, Mel, had been the stately centerpiece of the parade, riding matched palomino horses as part of a western equestrian

Dorothy Armitage on Route 66 near Vega, holding an unidentified child. *Author photo.*

group, the horses in silver-studded tack, the riders in decorative chaps and boots, unfettered scarves around their necks. With Carrie gone, would Mel ride? If he rode alone, a palpable grief would ride beside him for all to see. How and when did my unathletic Mother saddle up, coax her five-foot, one-inch frame onto the horse, and practice doing something she feared? But there she was, to the surprise of everyone, upright, even managing to hold the organization's flag, dressed in Carrie's western fringed outfit—a white Stetson smartly on her head—side by side with Mel, leading the parade. Mercifully, the palomino was old, too, and showed no signs of mustering the energy to buck her off.

The cowgirls I played with as a child have long since married and moved off to their downstate urban lives. As girls we played in the barns and in the "backyards" of ranch houses—the unfenced prairies and breaks. Tomboys, we rode horses, climbed haystacks, ate cattle cake up in the barn (it was molasses sweet), befriended whatever animals we could. We caught horny toads, bull and garter snakes, and ground squirrels, poor things. When my girlfriends were sent off to a prestigious boarding school in Dallas, I missed them, but I turned down the same opportunity so I could keep riding horses, playing basketball and clarinet, staying close to the natural world I'd grown up in. I finally gave up riding in my early college years, when a rank colt I'd been given reminded me that my bones could be broken. He made a fool of me one day, circling and circling until he lay down, almost crushing my leg.

I should have recognized my own melodrama from a long way off since I came by it so pervasively, not only attempting to be a cowgirl but steeped in the cowboy films of my childhood. One of my earliest memories is of the dark interior of Vega's downtown movie theater—a long, narrow room in a stone building where there were hard wooden benches and popcorn in brown bags brought from home and the flickering black and white film. How impressive the later color films were, but when I saw *Crazy Horse* I questioned the fake blood on the fake Indians used to dramatize the already inflated stories of the nineteenth-century West. I wanted Dale Evans to be more independent, too, and thus identified with Roy Rogers instead, asking for a birthday costume complete with red boots and six-shooters. Then there were Gene Autry and The Lone Ranger, which led to records, sheet music, and magic rings.

I am only a stucco house away from caves, dugouts, adobe dwellings, and migratory stone settlements—all remnants of the early plains people. In 1983, I moved from Albuquerque back to Vega, where I inherited a farmhouse on the edge of town from my great-aunt and -uncle. I moved in, with plans for a garden and orchard, and time to help my father with the family farm/ranch operation. My return to the land included fifty acres fronting a 1920 prairie-style bungalow, with a three-acre native pasture around it, and a New English–style barn I later discovered had been ordered from the Sears and Roebuck catalogue and assembled in 1926. When I moved in, I surveyed the old implements, the unopened Burpee seed packets left over from my uncle's gardening, and I examined the beds of iris, wild roses, and still-sprouting asparagus, the fifty-year-old peach tree—all hidden in weeds but once lovingly tended by my

Aunt Alice and Uncle Vern. Across town, my grandparents' house, which had been bought by a young couple, now recently divorced, had fallen into disrepair. Broken windows marred my granddad's workshop back of the house where he made furniture when I was a girl, propping the stump of his amputated leg on the lumber as he sawed. My grandmother's gardens lay forgotten under the kitchen window. Wanting to keep that generation's legacy alive, I clung more tenaciously to my house, which daily revealed forgotten treasures. In a rusted trunk in the root cellar, I discovered three quilts made by my great-grandmother, who at 101 years had still been sewing. What did it mean to sleep under these quilts again, to take in hand the rakes, hoes, scythes whose wood had lost its grain, smoothed by a generation's use?

My uncle had come from Chicago, where he worked for a printing company. Local farmers smirked at his farming practices, but he made a living, leaving behind this house and a small farm. The man who had built the house—Jess Giles—like many of the early generation of farmers to break out the plains in the Panhandle, had come from Tennessee when word of flat, potentially bountiful wheat country (and cheap land) reached them through the promotional literature of the developing railroad companies.

Jess Giles came to Texas with his family but moved out at age sixteen, building his own dugout south of town. When he earned enough money on the threshing crews, he bought a small acreage and built this house. Like so many men of his background and generation, he was, by necessity, a jack-of-all-trades. The house and barn are full of his wood-working projects: the five-inch baseboards, the cold frame for plants on the south side of the house, the windows situated for ventilation, the simple beveled glass in the front door— all suggesting ingenuity and grace. When the first telephone wires were strung in Oldham County on the existing cedar fence posts, Giles tried out the first connection in Vega by playing his fiddle into the wall phone. Uncle Vern bought the house and barn lot; he added more land and outbuildings. All are still standing, with slumped weather-worn doors and peeling stucco. The well house is a sign of the farm and house operations of that time: an elongated tub, hewn of cottonwood, held bottles of milk for cooling near the windmill, cold water piped from underground. I drink of this water still, although the windmill has been converted to a submergible pump. I think of these things as I listen to the drone of nearby Interstate 40, only a pasture away. For if the town grew up around the railroad in 1903, and Route 66 intersected the town in the 1930s, Interstate 40 most recently skirted south through my uncle's farm, the highway department paying him a scant thousand dollars for the right-of-way.

On many east-west trips I've driven this highway, which shadows not only the celebrated Route 66 but also the original Indian trails and later wagon trails in the area. The juxtaposition of dwelling places and migratory trails seems appropriate, nexus in a land said by early Anglo military and expeditionary explorers to be "empty," "uninhabitable," a useless "sea of grass": the "Great American Desert." Cruising through this country today, a traveler may experience only the impression of color, atmosphere, the dominance of sky, until, west of Adrian, you drop dramatically off what the early Spanish explorers called the *ceja*, an eyebrow of the llano escarpment. Measured in only human terms, the land seems monotonously open, arid, unworthy of love.

As I end my morning's winter walk, five miles north of I-40 from where I started, I like to think of the migrations of western box turtles, from bar ditch to bar ditch across this county road, which I've observed in early summer, and of tarantulas in early spring. The persistently digging badgers in winter course the hardpan caliche on the roadside, leaving deep potholes, sometimes undermining the softer fence rows. I think of the old bull we had who jumped fences, leaving hide behind. I've come upon avocets seining the runoff from windmills, sandhill cranes feeding in the milo stubble late fall. Antelope materialize in wheat fields in winter, disappearing over the horizon into the breaks if someone like me appears. This is another drought season, but even without rain, flint fragments surface among the small road rocks, beauties in their pink, white, and gray striations. True, these prairies invite migrations, crossings. I count the seasons by when the golden-headed blackbirds line the north-south fences, the bobolinks whirl in and out of the fields, the Swainson's hawks hunt, before the long migration to South America. Sandhill cranes leap into their mating dances in February. Monarchs searching out roadside milkweeds where they lay their eggs mark late August. They migrate, but they return.

I'm told by an observant friend that the cranes migrate at night by identifying the illumined neon gas station and fast-food signs. They migrate, they return, they adapt.

I was in my late fifties before I saw an official Soil Conservation Service map showing that the Middle Alamosa Creek heads in the South Draw of our place. I had never thought of the draws as the origin of an ancient streambed. I was surprised even more when I saw by the map that the Middle Alamosa emptied into the Canadian River right by Ysabel's Camp. A sheepman who moved from Anton Chico, Territory of New Mexico, to the salubrious Canadian valleys around 1877, Ysabel was one of the original pastores and later cowboys in the area, the cow camp named for him. My dad met Ysabel, already an old man, when Dad moved with his family to Vega at age sixteen. Dad talked a lot about Ysabel, I remember, but I can't recall any specifics, just a feeling. Seeing that mapped connection between my dad's place and Ysabel's, I immediately wanted to track the arc of their stories, Armitage Farms to Ysabel's Camp, back in time, yes, but in the cacophony of time and space made place, simultaneously moving forward following the deepening cuts of the Middle Alamosa Creek to see what the land might say. Maybe it would tell me of continuities rather than fragmentations.

Mary Austin believed that the rhythm and substance of Native American chants mirror a "landscape line"—that recitations, expressive human culture, echo local physical places. I wanted to find and follow that line.

And so the summers of hikes began.

There is persistence in this habit of landscape, this llano lyric, if in catching the motion, you can hear the song.

CHAPTER ONE

Draws

Ed could as well have been whittling away on a spare twig as running
the snake down the hole at the side of my house: the gesture was the
same. Years back his daddy, slim pocket knife in hand, had shaped an
after-lunch toothpick from a tree limb along with stories in front of
Swanson's grocery store—a regular. Now his son shucked the black
line into the sewer. He said: "Yeah. Your mom is a wonderful woman.
She was my Sunday school teacher, you know."
   I knew. This was an Ed-repeat, an old story, one he cherished telling and retelling. Probably no one knew exactly what it meant, but
for Ed, motherless and gay in the conservative Texas Panhandle, it
meant he was loved. And he loved my mother.
   My dad had recommended Ed even though he was the only
plumber in town. He had warned me too.
   "Don't let him come in the house if some of those guys are with him."
   "But Dad, most plumbers have to work inside your house."
   "Well, what I mean is, don't let those guys he drags along in."
   Dad was referring to Ed's habit of bailing out attractive young men
from the Amarillo jail and putting them to work for him.
   Ed was round as an apple, dressed in a red jumpsuit, and about
half the height of the two gaunt young men who fetched tools for him
from his truck.
   We had managed to be mostly outside, Ed sitting on my back deck,
legs dangling above the ground, lacing orders in between reminiscences.
   "She helped me with the newspaper too." He was turning earnest
now, no humor intended, though most folks familiar with the
long-gone Oldham County *News* might smile if it were compared

to a real newspaper. Small town newspapers covered births, deaths, Saturday afternoon baseball leagues, and garage sales. Even the current Vega paper sported a front page "The Sheriff's Report," detailing what thugs had been apprehended along Route 66 and how. "Sheriff and deputies pursued the suspect along the service road at high speeds until an arrest could be made" . . . or something like that.

I could feel safe about Route 66, now Interstate 40, which bordered my property on the south. A supposed meth lab, rumored to be located somewhere in Vega, worried me more.

"You remember Cleve Pattengail?" Maybe now Ed was warming to some gossip or another time-worn story.

"Yes, Daddy said he used to come in the bank."

"Yep. He carried a tow sack full of money and once a month walked to town to deposit it in the bank. He had a baby grand piano in that old country shack he lived in, and he let the animals on his place come and go. Last time I was there, the chickens were roosting on the piano."

I tried to image the old bachelor hunched into the wind, sack over his shoulder, walking the two miles from out in the country, plopping the bag down on my dad's desk at the bank to make a deposit. Cleve was dead now, and only a derelict, broken-bladed windmill stood by his collapsing shotgun house.

"What about Dutch Ruhl? Seems like he was an interesting old guy too?"

"Oh, Dutch. If he didn't like you he would bray like a donkey. If he did like you he did the same thing. He would just open his mouth as wide as he could and let out a holler. But that newspaper. Now there were some stories . . ."

⋎ I saw the first stages of the tearing down of Ed's old press office years later, after Ed had passed and when I was back in town for the summer vacation from university teaching. James was at it—forcing a tractor blade into one leaning wall. He was my high school boyfriend, the one who'd refused to help cut down the basketball net when his team, from nearby Adrian, beat Vega in district—all because we were dating. He's straddled loyalties ever since, working in both towns, but now it was part of Vega he was taking down. Though small—with barely enough room for the stout handpress— the building resisted. This had been the Oldham County *News*, the one Ed talked about.

A few months later, I drove past the vacant and weed-choked lot. Already an imitation "barn" building, made of pressed wood with faux carriage house appointments, sat for sale, fronting Ed's dilapidated barn out back. Ed's press ended up at the hardware store, where owner Randy Roark collects Oldham County antiques. Ed's estate is as enigmatic as his habits were. A stranger from out of town, said to be his partner, was named in his will to inherit everything.

Maybe that's what happened to his tombstone. A few years ago I saw it—a large decorative gray stone with his name big enough to be seen from the street—in front of an antique store in Amarillo. For sale. The fact is, Ed had two headstones. One is at the Vega cemetery where he is buried. The other was out in the country north of town on a piece of farmland he owned. You could see it from the highway. He wanted to be buried out there, but state law prohibited it. Had he bought two gravestones to be sure? Had his lover hocked the country stone, which originally faced toward the Canadian River breaks north of town, to sell to a dealer on tourized Route 66 in Amarillo? It seemed oddly appropriate to round the corner onto that street of the old Mother Road and see Ed's name among the antiques, memorabilia, the forgotten stories.

V Ed was right about the newspaper business and stories. One summer when I was fourteen, I got a job at the Vega Enterprise for the summer, working with a college intern, Gretchen Pollard. Gretchen came the five hundred miles from Austin in her orange Opal Cadette. When my parents and I welcomed her the night of her arrival, she remarked she was thrilled that Vega was large enough to have a high-rise building. We looked at each other, then couldn't contain our laughter. "Gretchen," my dad said sobering, "that's a grain elevator." From then on my dad's nickname for Gretchen was "Dizzy Blond." Gretchen, a petite but well-endowed, outspoken, dusky-voiced bleached blond (she was a smoker), lived up to her name all summer. Like the time we invited her to New Mexico with us. She waved from her Opal and pulled off the road. My dad turned around and went back to where Gretchen stood with the car hood up.

"Uncle Bob" (that's what she called him), "there's smoke coming out I guess from under here." She took a drag from her cigarette and laughed a kind of deep embarrassed utterance.

"Have you checked the oil?"

"What's that?"

Sure enough, there was almost no oil left when he checked it. Gretchen confessed that this was the first time she had ever checked her oil—or even looked under the hood.

Gretchen and I thought we were crack reporters. I had my own column, "The Teenage View," green banner head and all. We scoured the roadways of Oldham County for story possibilities—such exciting features as interviews with ministers, old-timers, and almost anyone who would talk to us. The Vega weekly was run by a capable but alcoholic editor and his equally inebriated ad man, so that the copy was left to us, with a little help from Dolly Stone, an older woman whose main job was to man the front desk and telephone. If Gretchen was a dizzy blond, Dolly was the proverbial battle axe. We feared her and took our morning tea breaks at Ollie's café across the street, returning right on the dot. Dolly came from a big family so she knew how to manage things. "Mighty, Dolly, Madge, and May, Marguerite, and Lula Clay," her father would intone, to remember the birth order of his six sizeable daughters.

One day when Bob, the editor, had actually come in to pick up copy, we had some questions and, not seeing him, asked where he had gone. Dolly huffed: "How would I know? He left out of here liked a ruptured duck."

Ruptured duck? We never figured out what that meant. And Bob never showed up again that day.

⋎ But these days, with Ed and his paper gone and the current Vega *Enterprise* moved down the street—managed by a woman who serves as owner, operator, reporter, and ad person—who remembers such stories? Or tells them? Where are they—and we—grounded?

Leslie Marmon Silko, the Laguna Pueblo writer, says "We are nothing without the stories." I think she means, literally, that if we don't know our cultural stories, we don't exist. But more: if we don't know where we fit into our cultural stories, then we have no identity, or "place." We are ungrounded. The southwestern writer Mary Austin famously created in her autobiography the "I-Mary," an identity realized when as a girl she understood her nature separate from her mother, relating intimately to her surrounding environment. Perhaps identity is founded upon our awareness of the "I" as we perceive it, not solely within but outside of ourselves: seeing ourselves in a larger story.

When I drive the three miles northwest of Vega to the family farm—a combination of farmed and native grassland—I sometimes catch the stoned looks of passersby, setting their cruise controls for top speed. The long horizon, 360 degrees of earth and sky, mostly grass, offends, disgusts, or just simply bores many people. Once when I was living in Albuquerque, a visiting friend from back East surveyed the then largely undeveloped northeast heights area and remarked: "Shelley, we've got to fill all this in."

I rock along in my 1987 Jeep Comanche pickup, aware that the perceived flatness is really, at four thousand feet, one of the largest plateaus in North America. Larger than the state of Illinois and encompassing parts of New Mexico and Texas and east almost into Oklahoma, from the Canadian River north to almost the Edwards Plateau south, the caprock (as it is called for the caliche-like Ogallala formation) was laid down in the Pleistocene. It's going to be quite a challenge to fill all this in. Within it, Oldham County, one of the larger in Texas, covers fifteen hundred square miles.

It's not some low-lying flatness, but a mountain of sorts, this plateau. Just to the north and farther west, the land slopes into draws, then shallow canyons, and finally deep cuts through time—inverted mountains. The sublime western landscape of mountainous New Mexico, Arizona, and especially California—possibly the destinations of these escaping tourists—is simply plunged into the earth here. What was substance, rising above, is now space slicing, yawning below. So locals know a thing or two the exasperated I-40 travelers don't: there's something out there. Space, yes, but it's not "empty"—rather it is filled with the mysteries of mountains turned upside down. Mainly, we know it's not flat.

But if the landscape is boring to those just passing through, wouldn't the local stories be boring too? Are our stories at most understories?

Most passers-through stories are about the weather. "Oh yeah, Vega. I was caught there in the most god-awful blizzard." "Yeah, my car broke down there. The one garage was closed on Saturday and Sunday. Wind blowing like hell." "OMG, that's the place we spent two days in somebody's home, put up with the other travelers when the two motels filled up."

I usually respond with an apologetic yes, then *my house, built in 1920, is the one along the highway with the red roofed barn—one of the few wooden barns left in the county,* but break off, losing my nerve to balance the stereotypes. Located on Interstate 40 or old route 66 and the intersecting state highway 385, which goes to Colorado, Vega is the last stop between Amarillo and Tucumcari, New Mexico, almost at the midpoint of Route 66. A Spanish name meaning meadow or pasture, Vega suggests why snowstorms can be dangerous here. Drifts and blinding snow frighten most visitors away. Old-timers and travelers agree on the well-worn tome: "There's nothing between here and the North Pole but a barbed wire fence." Or if they've been here a really long time, they like to brag about walking to school from out in the country, the snow so high they walked over fence posts without knowing it.

I lived through two massive blizzards myself in the 1950s. Stranded travelers filled schools and homes. One girl was airlifted out of a local home by helicopter due to complications with her polio. Local ranchers worried about their livestock. For kids like me a blizzard meant staying at home from school and making lots of snow ice cream, since all my brother and I had to do was open his bedroom window and scoop up the snow. The house was buried in snow all the way up to the windowsills.

Donnie Allred, the county judge, likes to tell about his grandfather who lived south of Wildorado, a town of about 180 people east of Vega. One of his stories recalls a time when his grandfather's young wife was pregnant with their first child. He took the train to Amarillo to get some supplies, planning to stay overnight. But a severe snowstorm hit while he was gone. This is characteristic of an area where it's not uncommon to see daily fifty-degree swings in the temperature. When he tried to get back home, the train was not running. He tried renting a horse from a livery stable but no one would let a horse in that kind of weather.

Finally, in order to get back to his wife, Donnie's grandfather decided to walk from Amarillo, some twenty miles today by interstate. By that time, the storm was really a blizzard: snow accumulating, low visibility. To keep from getting lost, he counted the steps between the first two telephone poles, which ran along the railroad. He then counted his steps between each successive pole. If he reached the end of his steps and there was no pole, he knew he was lost. He would then retrace his steps and try again.

When he got home, he was snow-blind for three days. "Some Indian who worked out at Gray's ranch north of Wildorado got wind of his ailment," Donnie added. "He came in and made a poultice and Granddad got his vision back."

Donnie made a good point the day I sat in his judge's office, with local brands displayed and spurs hanging on the wall. The people of Oldham County and Vega are only one generation removed from the "Old West." My dad's generation was the glue between the earliest settlers and the living generation—ours, people in their sixties and younger. For at least these two generations the local stories still make sense. They create a common ground.

One reason might be the compression of time here. Unlike New England or other areas of the Southwest, here the settlement pattern is recent. Until the 1880s, there was no incorporated town or county seat in Oldham County. Vega was incorporated as a town in 1904; Tascosa in 1880 as the original county seat. The end of the so-called Old West and the burgeoning wind energy generation are separated by a little more than one hundred years.

Turns out my dad knew the second non-Native settler in the area—Ysabel Gurule, who came from Anton Chico, New Mexico (then the Territory of New Mexico) as one of the first pastores, sheepmen who discovered the Canadian River Valley, north of Vega about twenty miles. Born in 1863, Ysabel came when he was sixteen, traveling with his cousin and family from the Pecos River Valley. When he built his dugout near the Canadian banks, America had hardly survived the Civil War. The last Native holdouts from the reservation in Oklahoma—a small band of Comanche, some Kiowa—still threatened settlers, though the tribes had been broken by Ranald Mackenzie's surprise attack of the then three thousand remaining Comanche, Kiowa, and other tribes in nearby Palo Duro Canyon. Ysabel's cousin was killed by Indians near the Canadian and his wife returned to Anton Chico, but Ysabel stayed. In the free unfenced grasslands of that time, the pastores sought out the rich grasses in the valleys along the Canadian, establishing their plazas near springs.

Dad also came to the Panhandle when he was sixteen. Forced from their farm near the confluence of the White and the Buffalo Rivers in the Mississippi flood of 1926, the Armitages resettled in Vega, coming for the promise of the rich wheat harvests in the recently broken out prairie in the western Panhandle. Ysabel must have been around sixty-three years old when the Armitages moved to Vega, still a cowhand at the LS ranch. He died in 1936. By that time, Dad was a teller at First State Bank. What transpired between them I'll never know.

What I do know is Dad talked a lot about Ysabel; maybe he identified his own new start with Ysabel's. Bit by bit Dad had begun buying farm and grassland—land that went for three dollars an acre then—beginning in 1929. Ysabel witnessed the conversion of the vast free grasslands, still shared by buffalo, into large fenced ranches and smaller farms. The conversion of the open plains to private ownership meant the end of the pastores, who mostly returned to New Mexico. Ysabel stayed and became a crack cowboy. I think Dad saw in Ysabel the embodiment of the spirit of adventure and also his knack for adapting to the changes.

He might have had a bit of the old-time West in him too, my dad. At twenty-one, then a new teller at the First State Bank in Vega, he was to be married on November 24, 1932, to eighteen-year-old Dorothy Mae Dunn from Amarillo, Texas. At noon, on November 15, he was kidnapped during a bank robbery. Most of the employees had gone to lunch and Dad was locking up to join them. Two armed, masked (yes!) men came in, took the cash available at the teller's cages, locked two employees in the bank vault, blindfolded Dad, bound his hands behind his back with rope, and threw him into the

Ysabel Gurule at dugout on (Middle) Alamosa Creek.

back of their automobile. The get-away ensued, the robbers finally stopping the car about nine miles southeast of Amarillo. There was mumbling in the front seat, then a slamming of doors. Dad heard another car start up and drive away.

In some Houdini way, he contorted his six-foot-plus frame until he managed to open the door. Realizing the robbers had ditched the car off the road, he assumed there was a fence nearby. There was: a barbed-wire fence. He rubbed the rope against the barbs until he was free, then set about hot-wiring the car, started it up, drove into Amarillo, and reported to the Sheriff's Department that the bank had been robbed and he had been kidnapped.

The sheriff's deputy on the desk looked more than a little surprised. They had just received word that two armed and dangerous kidnappers had robbed the bank in Vega. And here was the young hostage standing before their eyes. The next day, the newspaper report carried the story with a goofy-looking photograph of my dad, who looked as though it had all been great fun. As I look at the picture now, I see a resemblance to my jokester brother. Jibes made the rounds in Vega, the best one from one of Dad's good friends. "Bob,"

R. A. Armitage (*second from right*), First State Bank, Vega, Texas. *Author photo.*

he said, "Surely to goodness if you didn't want to get married, there was an easier way."

I talk to the cowboys around here. One of them is my neighbor, James Henry, known as "Frog." I can hear him switching out trailers, moving cattle and horses, in the early mornings and in the evening. He's still a strapping six feet, fit, checkered work shirt, Levis, and piss-stained boots. When I pass we hang out in his driveway and talk.

"Hear about Willie Shipp getting struck by lightning?" he asks, as casual as ordering a local hamburger.

"What?? The lightning struck you?" Frog is soft-spoken. I missed what he said.

"Nope. Willie. You know, Willie Shipp. Hit his hat, went down his back straight through the saddle. Killed the horse. Sent Willie to the hospital for a few days. He really liked that old saddle. And the horse too, of course."

I heard later Willie actually had been struck twice by lightning.

Talk about being grounded.

I run into the guy who runs cattle on our place, Sam Brown, about a week later.

"What's the news?" I ask, hoping for a cougar sighting or antelope herd report, but no hospitalized cowboys.

"Got bucked off last week," he drawls, rubbing a weathered jaw. I notice his raw-looking hands settled on the pickup door, bunged up and chapped.

"Broke a rib," he continues.

"My gosh. Sam, you and Willie need to stay away from those horses."

"Hard to do when you have spent your life on one."

Sam's a college graduate, has written several western novels, won awards. He used to deliver mail on the country route in a beat up Chevy Geo—anything to give him time to write and to cowboy. But his agent began pressing for more books. The fun of it went out for him. He bought a few head of cattle, mostly stopped writing, and kept working for the ranches when they needed day help.

I want Sam to keep writing the stories. He's got an insider's view. I realize how much I am on the edge of such things, a single woman who works somewhere else, who now mainly summers here. I want to know what Sam knows but am not about to ask. Call it shyness or the clear knowledge that it's mostly a man's world out there. Somebody once said to him: "Sam, there must be so many stories to tell about cowboying and the ranch life." To which he replied: "Yeah, if you could repeat them." How could I ever be privy to those stories? More than that, how could I subtly coax them out of him? But I know ranch history, the cowboy era, is not the only story here. And there's something about sensing the edges of experience that's a kind of truth in itself.

Edges—the kind of selvage a seamstress might toy with. That's what it's like to stop at the north boundary of our land on the cusp of the Canadian Breaks—a rough country of deep washes, canyons, and juniper breaks stretching all the way to the Canadian River. Here the relatively level farmland gives way to inflections of purple canyons, ochre- and rose-striated arroyos. To be on the edge of these is most profound. Nothing is given away and surprises await. Like a good story, there's the anticipation of the twists and turns, no spoiler alert needed—a kind of growing perception that is itself an experience.

I want to believe this because the middle generation—the glue, as Donnie said—and most of their landmarks are gone. And that fickle twin of truth—memory—is not identical but wayward. I have snippets, like the cassette tape I made of Bea Godwin playing the Vega Methodist Church organ when she was an old lady. I remember Bea's hands looking a lot like Sam's—puffed with arthritis, swollen tight against her wedding ring. Bea had long been our organist and accompanist for musical events in Vega. She transposed sheet music, like "Somewhere Over the Rainbow," so my not quite soprano, not quite alto voice could manage the high notes. Her parlor, where both a piano and a foot-pedal organ sat, was often papered with sheets of road tunes, popular hits, big band numbers. That must be why when I hear the first stanzas of "It Had to Be You" or some other standard from before my time, I can sing the lyrics. That, and the fact that my parents owned all those old 78s. But Bea's claim to fame, as far as I am concerned, was that at age thirteen she was asked to fill in at a theater in her native Chicago, playing the pit organ for a vaudeville show. Not even five feet tall then, she could barely reach the organ pedals to play. I look at her hands somehow still reaching over an octave despite their stumpy shape, and I listen. When at church she played "The Old Rugged Cross," there was a doodly-do between notes. I smile. Her ragtime days shone through.

No less an accomplished memoirist than Patricia Hampl notes that memoir is not factual, not about what happened, but about the shape of memory. Emotional truth, that keeper, sets our feet—as flat and forgettable as the ground might seem to some—and we write on.

ᐯ That ground, our land, is memorably shaped. Far from flat, both the North and South Places are distinguished by grass-covered draws, though the North Place is rougher. On the South Place the draw slopes gently after the initial cut in the land, which runs from under Interstate 40, widening to maybe two hundred yards across. The bottom—some seventy-five yards from the smooth edges—is carpeted, even in winter, in native prairie gramas and forbs. Plants as tiny as the pink-lipped and shaggy-leafed "frog hair" and the taller, royal purple ironweed cluster in the water-collecting bottomland. According to our family friend Mildred Hicks, our farm was beautiful because it had two draws on it. Unlike the Hicks's farm, mostly flat irrigated land, ours had natural contours and untilled native grasses.

This compliment came from a woman whose father homesteaded the large lucrative spread she spent her life on, south of Vega. The Hicks had irrigated farmland, and it was extremely productive. They drove top-of-the-line Chryslers while my parents owned a Plymouth. Mildred told stories of gathering the mail left by a sort of Pony-Express mailman who stashed it between two rocks out in the country. She kept her parents' saddles prominently displayed in her house—and oiled. She reminded me that our place—dry land farm that it was—was native grass too. And that it had draws.

A draw is a cleavage in the landscape. Mike Harter, an Amarillo high school honors history teacher, is an expert on draws in the West Texas and eastern New Mexico region. He makes detailed, hand-drawn maps locating the major draws and indicating their relationship to tributaries of the Canadian River, the only river in this arid area. I met him at a coffee shop in Amarillo where he unscrolled a couple of maps, pointing.

"Here in West Texas and in eastern New Mexico people use the term 'draw' to describe creek beds that wander through the landscape. Farther west, the proper word might be 'arroyo' or 'wash,' but 'draw' is appropriate here on the High Plains. A draw suggests that the terrain must somehow coax scarce moisture into its course."

I eyed a tiny section along I-40 where part of a wishbone-shaped figure indicated the two draws on our farm.

"Yeah, we used to get twenty inches average rainfall a year, and now I bet it's half of that, right?"

He nodded, repeating the old Panhandle conundrum that if you don't like the weather here just wait five minutes and it will change. But we both knew the constants are wind and the pervasive absence of water. So draws are those essential collectors and conveyers of water.

The draw on our South Place, the one along I-40 on the south, greens in summers with short and hardy buffalo grass, side oats grama, blue grama, and various forbs. It winds from the southwest section of the land to the northeast, where it continues over into neighbor Kim Montgomery's ranch, beginning as a slim cut then widening to a middle expanse of perhaps a quarter mile across. The entire draw may snake a mile or so from fence to fence. I think of it like the rounded backs of two gigantic dinosaurs, the humps smooth and benign, drawing the eye softly. Vegetarian, like the brontosaurus. The strip of greener grasses at the bottom, dotted with purple iron weed and white Queen Anne's lace in summer, reveal the drawing of water too.

At the north part of the farm, about two and a half miles north (the highway or South Place and the North Place are divided by two other small farms), the North Draw runs from the southwest to the northeast. I think of it more as a carnivore. The banks are ruddy in eroded soil and clay and the cut more severe, more intent in its pull toward the river. Rather than meander it devours the less stable soils, a jagged mouth waiting to consume anything that passes along the drop in elevation. Here are native grasses, but also broom weed, from drought cycles and overgrazing, bear grass, yucca, and what I like to call my cactus forest. It's on fairly level ground before the first pitch of the draw—a cluster of six-foot-tall cholla, a lingering reminder of the biota of this ranchland before it was cleared for farming. Farther south of here in the irrigated country, people burn and poison the chollas. If there's a grass fire some folks rejoice that "at least it's burned down the cholla." I smile when I see the small, rounded heads emerge from the blackened ground again. A water collector, it's home to the cactus wren and the yucca moth. In the bad old days of drought, cattlemen burned only the thorns so the cattle could eat the arms for moisture. This North Draw becomes the wilder of the two as the soil type changes, a precursor to the badlands beyond.

The two draws connect, the crux of the wishbone on Mike's map, beyond Armitage Farms over on Green's ranch as they join other tributaries on the run north.

I never thought about this connection of our place to the next when I was a girl. Fences tend to do that. The illusion of ownership. Besides, I was too busy doing things like learning to drive.

I learned to drive on the humpback of the old South Draw. Kids get their licenses in Oldham County at age fourteen, but they learn to drive "in the country" at much younger ages. I was seven years old when I first got behind the wheel.

We were in the 1947 International pickup. I liked it because that was year of my birth. I thought of it as a friend until I tried to drive it.

The excuse was feeding cattle cake, the elongated pellets of molasses and pressed grains, to the winter herd. I was helping my daddy at the farm; out of his good graces he said so. I was always eager to help my dad, so learning to drive was important. I can still see myself in the dark green pickup, head barely level with the black steering wheel, seat cushions stacked so I could see over it. The long-necked shift fronted the bench seat. I liked the feel of the soft plastic knob, malleable, a guide, a tool, to be cupped in my sweaty hands.

My dad chose to teach me to drive on the smooth cusp of the South Draw. I might as well have been looking out of a space shuttle; a whole unknown world seemed poised in the air below. The pickup pointed slightly down the slope, ready to buck and pitch at any slip of the clutch.

"Now put your foot on the brake," he instructed, matter of factly in what I thought was a life-and-death situation. "Keep the clutch down, and ease off the brake. Here, I'll put it in neutral first and you can just ease it down the hill. I'll be in the back tossing out cake."

What kind of a crazy daddy was this? In the back. Tossing out cake. Me in the cab. Alone. The cattle bunched around the truck, slobbering on my window, bawling so loud I could barely hear. We both knew I would have to master the clutch. I sweated beneath my Peter Pan bangs. I heard a suction sound from my wet armpits.

"You just ease off the brake and steer straight downhill until I yell stop."

By now the cattle had completely surrounded the truck. They bellowed and begged and blocked my way.

"But won't I run over the cattle? . . ."

Dad persisted in his instructions. There were too many of them and all at once: I've got the brake on. See if you can reach the brake pedal. No, that's the clutch. Here's let's try first gear and you just gradually let the clutch out. You've got to keep your other foot on the brake until you do.

My stomach clutched like it does at night when you think you hear something scratching at the window and even if you know there's only a bush out there, you gulp at the shadow.

I tried several times. I eased the clutch out. The pickup died. It lurched forward. It died. My dad was a tall man with long arms and legs, a kind of Hollywood hero in my mind. He seemed larger than life, like a western movie star. When he reached over the wheel to correct me or straddled the gear shift knob to hit the brakes when I popped the clutch—all this in our practice sessions—he made me nervous. I didn't want to make mistakes or disappoint. I wanted to help my daddy. I wanted to keep coming to the farm with him.

Finally, we got to the point where he left me alone, the truck in gear, the toes of one foot pointed like an earnest dancer, depressing the clutch pedal, the other flat on the foot brake. He climbed back into the truck bed where the feed sacks were—oh trust, oh terror, oh dangerously living daddy. He said he would yell when it was time for me to stop. I managed to look up from the dizzying mantra of "how-to's" and glimpse him in the rearview mirror saying something back. But I couldn't hear him. How would I know when to stop?

Memory is a strange thing. How much is the lingering sense of things, a kind of felt thought? There was a piercing whistle at one point. I stopped. I was right on the edge where the draw pitched to its more rugged bottom. To this day, if anyone whistles, I snap my head, I brake, I stop.

⩔ There were other edges too. My brother, Roy, learned to drive up and down the draw, but he also got to drive the tractor—by himself. Early on I got the idea of what boys get to do and girls don't. But why couldn't you inhabit both worlds, I wondered, and besides the man's world seemed so much more interesting than cooking up a recipe in a hot kitchen. It wasn't that Dad thought I couldn't do the work; he knew how hard it was. He was liberal for his time, taking me out to play golf when I was thirteen, dragging out an old wooden tennis racket to exchange strokes back and forth across the tennis net. We both knew in small-town Texas you could run for Miss Oldham County one night and play basketball the next. Yes, he put that basketball goal up in the yard. Still, my brother drove the tractor, a boring and sleep-inducing job before air conditioners and radios in the cabs. When our cousin Jimmy visited, the temptation was too much for the two of them, and Dad found them one day running down the planting rows by the moving tractor, chasing each other around it, trying to see how long it would stay straight in the row without a driver.

I finally did get to drive the tractor. I plowed one summer when Roy was off working as a smoke jumper in Idaho. The boys had set a tone for goof-offs and sometimes goof-ups, even though they eventually got their work done, but no matter how hard I tried to get it right, at day's end there was always an uneven place in the field, where the plow had not been set right. One day a rainstorm came up and by the time I could get the tractor back to the gate to get off, I was soaked and the plow balled up in the mud. Now the field was really uneven! Lightning rocketed nearby; I made a dash for the truck. I had on cutoffs and the rain and mud splashed and stuck to my legs and tennis shoes. In town, only three miles away, it had not rained. I went to my parents' house to report the situation. Rather than entering in my muddy state, I rang the doorbell. My dad opened the door, expecting to see a visitor rather than a daughter who looked like she'd just come from a mud wrestling contest. "What the hell . . . ?" he trailed off. This from a man who rarely uttered a cuss word around Mother and me.

⋁ When you're a kid you don't think you have a story. You spend your time trying to find yourself in someone else's. So I loved our farm but coveted the ranches out north, the beguiling canyons and seemingly infinite horizons from the North Place. What would it be like to grow up like the Mansfield daughters on their ranch? There are 640 acres in a section; Dad owned not quite two sections, a small part that was leased.

Tom Green's ranch, joining our place on the north, was a fairyland to me. Some kids believed in fairies. I had visions of discovering dinosaur bones, an Indian mano and metate, or of glimpsing a shifty bobcat on the prowl. When we visited the Greens' place, everything seemed exotic compared to town. Tom fed wild turkeys out back, quail scattered when you drove up, there were ranch dogs and horses to ride. Tom Henry, the Greens' son, had some sort of mechanical horse, which we kids took turns riding. In town, my favorite "toy" as a child was a wooden horse, handmade, suspended on springs which let you rock away like crazy. Even the yard to the Greens' was an adventure: there were all sorts of native plants, "horny toads," rattlesnakes possibly lurking to keep us properly scared.

And at Margaret and Marilyn Mansfield's home on the ranch north of Tom Green's, the original headquarters for one of the oldest ranches in the area (the headquarters now on the Historic Registry), they had haylofts for hide and seek and an elegant historical house built of imposing Canadian River stone. We kids would hang out in the hay, nibbling cattle cake like it was a candy bar. The Mansfields had a maid, and on a hot summer day you could come in, go barefoot onto the cooling stone floors, and be served lemonade. To me, Margaret and Marilyn were the luckiest girls in the world: they were raising orphaned antelope twins on a bottle in the back corral.

Later both girls went to private schools in Dallas, marrying investment bankers and eventually selling their parts of the ranch, which included the historic ranch house built from two bunk houses modeled after the picture on an Arbuckle coffee can. I left too, but to a state university near Dallas and later to one a two-hour drive away, returning for holidays and summers.

They had the Canadian Breaks, cactus and mesquite-studded grasslands, creeks, a river. We had draws.

One day my dad picked me up at school with the refrain I loved—"Let's go to the farm." He said we were going out to take down an old barbed wire fence that couldn't be repaired. It was rusty old wire, slack in places, broken, so he was replacing sections of it when he had time. His "day job" was as vice president of First State Bank, but throughout his working life he rose early, put on a blue work shirt, and went to the farm. He came back in, changed to a starched white shirt with tie, and put in a day at the bank. After hours, he again changed to the work shirt and headed for the farm.

That day he told me the story of the wire and the XIT ranch. Once the largest range in the world, three million acres—XIT standing for "Ten in Texas," referring to the ten counties of the Texas Panhandle that it covered—the XIT also had the largest pasture when the land was first fenced. Our fence was now part of this pasture, one that had stretched some twenty miles to the Canadian River. The wire was thick, about a half-inch wide, with formidable barbs. We wound the wire up and later stored some of it in my barn, where a stray cat decided to hide her new litter of kittens. As we took the fence down I finally realized: the land is bounded by memories, even mine.

But when I started trying to tell stories by writing them, they still weren't my stories. I thought you had to imagine something more exotic than what was to be found at home. My grade school friend Cynthia and I, both lovers of the Hardy Boys and Nancy Drew, decided to write our own mystery novel the summer before the sixth grade. We dutifully recorded our tale in penciled hand on the yellowed pages of a large wooden-bound book her mother had. There were no ranches, no draws. To aid our imaginations, which at that time were wrapped in ruin and mystery (we were both lovers of Poe), we set the novel in a real-life setting: the abandoned but once mansion-like house of Colonel Owens, an early settler and booster of Oldham County.

We would sneak out of Cynthia's house at night, under the pretenses of my spending the night, and with trepidations that made us whisper and giggle made our way to Colonel Owens's dilapidated house. What we hoped—or feared—we'd find there, I don't know. We peered in the broken windows, eyeing the still perilously hanging chandelier. One time we climbed in the window and tried the rickety stairs to the upper story, where I am sure we thought we'd find a skeleton or two. Our novel's villain, sad to say, was Tony, a mentally challenged man in Vega who often materialized at the drug store or grocery store. We all loved Tony, really, but he scared us too; in real life he jumped out from corners or from around buildings, saying "Boo" in a deep voice. In our novel, he was about the nicest villain you could think of.

In elementary school, I kept writing about the other Wests, as if they were more important than my own. I started two "novels," one about a cowboy and his kid sister. "Down the old dusty street of Seigebrush [sic] a horse trotted. It wasn't just any horse, it was Benson Taylor's horse. He was the biggest and most feared outlaw in the whole south-west," etc. The other was about a Chinese boy's life with his laundry-owning parents.

Where did these stereotypes come from? Likely "Li-Yung and His Lucky Kite," as well as Cowboy Drew and Sis Sherry, came to me courtesy of the early black-and-white westerns on television, where stereotypes abounded. I think the Chinese story came from questions about a brass box on my dad's desk said to be Chinese and for the "lucky cricket." We had lots of crickets in those days in our house—built in the early 1920s, remodeled but keeping true to its wood frame, with uneven baseboards and slightly akimbo door facings. The crickets always slipped in, showing up along baseboards, surprising us in the chest of drawers—deadly, omnivorous pests to be whacked by my fly-swatter-toting mother. The invasion of the crickets signaled all-out war in the summers. To be saved in the lucky box meant the cricket was lucky indeed.

The glassed-in porch, my dad's study on the front of the house, was supposedly off limits to my Mother's hodgepodge of clipped coupons, address books, and saved newspaper articles (although I later found all these stashed in a bottom drawer of the filing cabinet). But Dad let me write at his desk. I hoped that I would be inspired by my great aunt's published poetry books, his sets of colored pens, and the small pink portable typewriter.

The porch took on mystical proportions for me. One particular day on the porch—I think I was in the seventh grade—the porch felt sheltering, mainly because of the light. A winter light that seemed to hold us all in its breath—cold blue rising—filled the windows. Those days what is now a very busy Highway 385 was mostly empty. I remember the near silence, only the scraping of the lilac bushes in their wintry rasp on the side of the house, barely reaching the windowsill. It was a special feel of promise, somehow tied to comfort and home yet with yearning and even loneliness in it. Across the street at the Catholic parsonage where the priest kept peacocks, their raucous calls seemed suspended in the winter air—filling space as on a blank page.

One of the things I wrote there—aside from illustrated book reports (the review of *The Old Man and the Sea* bound by a shellacked fish skeleton; the *Ben Hur* report unfurled with coffee-stained and dirt-smudged paper mimicking papyrus)—was a letter of interest to *National Geographic*. My letter was an exceedingly naïve gesture but one that showed how much I wanted to write about the natural world, other landscapes, flora and fauna I was not only curious about but felt connected to. I wanted to be a writer. I wanted to write about the kinds of things that appeared in *National Geographic*. I was just trying to discover what kind of education, what training I needed.

Later, a form letter reply came, noting that its writers were professionals; in other words, You need not apply. My first pink slip. Would I ever amount to anything I deeply desired? The day of the rejection letter all journeys revealed themselves as detours. The blue hovered and held. Yet there was an inner joy that persisted, now tempered by a necessary kernel of defeat, especially when set against the exaggerated hopes dashed that day. My dad's desk remained sacrosanct, along with the farm, and after he died, it was the platform from which my mother paid the bills, ran the farm, until her own disabilities struck. Another edge—another not quite there.

⋎ One of my favorite childhood books was *The Edge of Time* by Loula Grace Erdman. It had a special place on the porch among my mother's Reader's Digest books, ordered monthly. I liked this novel because it was the only one I knew of set in the Texas Panhandle and it focused on a young married homesteading couple. Hardly the adventure script of the male western, it was a woman's story, realistic rather than romantic. The title intrigued me even then, and now the frayed cover on my bookshelf reminds me of that question Sarton posed after falling under the spell of the expansive Southwest. Why has this llano region not inspired a significant literature?

Why indeed? I think of Mike Harter's maps again and an article he wrote called "The Highways of the Plains." In it he explained how the Llano Estacado, the so-called Staked Plains, is a vast, flat plain that sheds its water stingily, mostly into playa sinks but also into draws that, he says, "are one of the few real drainages to be found here." Several theories exist about the origin and meaning of the llano, of which the great caprock is a part, but they all agree this "sea of grass" was formidable to travel, with miles and miles of seeming featureless prairie and precious few water sources. These great conduits, the draws, were water highways holding water below the surface, and during cloudbursts, conveying water downstream in instant floods called "high rises." More, they were highways for Native peoples, prehistoric and historic, because they provided shelter, possible water and food, and a route to water, as they held spring sites and culminated in the Canadian River. If pursued, a person could disappear into them.

In college I starting jogging for fitness. I jogged five miles a day for thirty years. I sought out softer soils for running, and when home I always ran at the farm. It became a local joke. "You still running?" someone would ask at the post office, eyeing my dusty shoes and worn out leggings. But the running taught me something. I began to learn that the land was lyric. I could feel the rhythm of its shape come into my legs, up into my chest and heart, and out my mouth as breath.

Later it came out as writing.

Mostly I ran along the edges of the draws, the more level wheat and milo fields on one side, the draws on the other. Later the asphalt of urban Honolulu claimed me after years of teaching and running there; arthroscopic surgery and worn out knees reduced me to a walk. To my surprise, walking was even more sonorous than running. I noticed things I had never seen before. Each walk was different. I felt like Barry Lopez, who says that after his thirty years of living on the same patch of land in Oregon he still finds something new. I took to the highway of draws.

This highway, I discovered, had a name. On Mike's map it was labeled the Middle Alamosa Creek. Further checking of topographic maps and a large land map at the county court house revealed it as an "intermittent creek." The Middle Alamosa is the central branch and largest of three Canadian River tributaries that empty into the Canadian about twenty miles north near the site of Tascosa.

There was one "alamosa"—or cottonwood—on our South Place, right in the middle of the widest expanse of the draw. And I knew along the Canadian and its valleys there were plenty of cottonwoods, some purposely planted by the early pastores for shade. Perhaps the Middle Alamosa got its name from the denser stand of trees near the river. Our single cottonwood was in its death throes. The standing water that sometimes surrounded it had no doubt rotted the roots. A porcupine could sometimes be seen napping on an upper limb—right above the raw strips where he had gnawed the bark, thus further weakening the hapless tree. Nevertheless, it was a testimony to water.

⋁ Middle Alamosa. I was amazed. According to the maps it headed on our land, right at what was Interstate 40—in the draw.

This explained the cracked concrete one-lane overpass near that highway. Parallel to what is now the interstate was a one-lane road called the Ozark Trail, starting in St. Louis and running to California, a precursor of Route 66. The overpass must have served as a water crossing. Earlier it had been an Indian trail, the Indians originating the best overland routes. I occasionally found flint from the Alibates Flint Quarry, northeast of Amarillo, suggesting this was a trade route—the red, white, and purple-streaked dolomite highly valued for its strength and beauty. The Ozark Trail was built and used primarily in the 1920s. The prehistoric and historic Indians traded from as early as the Clovis period (15000 B.C.E.) to the 1880s. Likely the Armitages traveled the Ozark Highway when it was the only roadway from Arkansas west into Vega. On one walk there I leaned over the pipe barrier on top and checked the swallow's nests underneath. After rains, cattle liked to stomp around in the shaded pooling underneath; tracks of antelope and skunk suggested other visitors. I liked to imagine what went on here at night when no one was looking.

Downstream, now that I could imagine it as one, the creek widened and a Civilian Conservation Corps (CCC) dam, concrete and native stone, hung perilously over eroded banks. Some corpsman had scratched "1936" into the concrete on top. I liked to swab up the Triops that slew in the muddy areas below. Their date of origin: circa three hundred million years ago to the present, Jurassic survivors. Dinosaur shrimp, some people call them. A living fossil, they have hardly changed since the Jurassic period. Their eggs can remain dormant for years, hatching only when there is sufficient water and proper temperature. Pentimento, you remind us that something always lives below, contemporary life a remnant in your twirling tentacles.

Catching and keeping: that's what folks tried to do with the water. My dad built yet another dam more recently behind the aging CCC one. Part of the reason was conservation for watering cattle, but he also stocked the pond with catfish, building a feeder he would send out into the waters, like Moses's basket into the bulrushes. After my dad's death, the rusting of the feeder, and droughts that dried the pond for years, I had forgotten the catfish. But after a rain, Triops like, I saw them flopping over the check dam, resurfacing in a wet

South Draw after a high rise. *Author photo.*

season. I tried to catch them with an old fishnet rummaged out of the garage to return them to the now-full pond. When most of them got away, I realized you can't stop the flow.

And yet the settlers had tried. Dams and fences and corrals and railroads and country roads. I, too, wanted to save something of my father, the emblem of his love of this place, by keeping the catfish from escaping with the water downstream. Tom Green, on the ranch just north, had a one-room camp where he used to escape to nap and read Paris Match. He had cookouts there and sometimes invited us out. The iron cookstove was a beauty and so heavy it took three men to wrestle it into its place. During one of the high rises—Tom's retreat is on the Middle Alamosa—the iron stove was washed away, later discovered mired in the muddy banks of the Canadian.

Water will have its way.

When my dad died our family's relationship to the land shifted. I still ran the roads but touched ground like you work a worry stone. My mother and I looked at each other and wondered how we would run the farm. My brother was in Omaha and later Houston, far away and already removed from the necessary knowledge of farm programs, grazing leases, and grain prices. I had only indirect

Dorothy Mae with harvester Carl Johnson. *Author photo.*

experience. Mother had driven a grain truck during the first harvests in the 1930s, grinding the gears in such a way that Dad said she took two inches off the roadway.

Hers was a mostly rosy view of the particulars—sunbaked skin, cow piss, and broken machinery—of running a small farm. When a PBS film crew came to record interviews with local survivors of the Dust Bowl, my mom's story was not the expected page out of the Grapes of Wrath. Rather than remember dust pneumonia, jack rabbit roundups, and Black Sundays, she told love stories. Her favorite (and mine): to get the farm work done, my dad had to plow by the tractor lights late at night, after he had gotten off work from the bank. She lovingly wound herself around his feet on the tractor platform, behind the pedals, to keep him company, sleeping as he wheeled through the dust into the night.

So for a while she manned the desk, running the farm by rarely going there. I went out to the farm with George Ramos, our hired hand, whose knowledge of the place was the only way we made it through the years after Dad died.

"See that soil," George would say, pointing to the course red soil in the North Place fields. George was a strong, barrel-chested man, but his gentle voice comforted me. "It's different from the highway place, balls up in the plow, harder to get a crop up on. It's great for grass, though," he laughed, "and bindweed and every other crawling thing that's not supposed to be in this field." We both knew the llano wanted to be grass and still resisted the plowing, spraying, and planting that made nesting night hawks flee. I plowed and George planted—his, the more precise art—and somehow we made it through the first season.

Sitting atop a tractor gave me a new perspective, maybe something like when white western women first sat a horse. It was an equalizer of sorts, but the view also made me think about how the North Draw had been the scene of deprivation, kidnapping, and murder. There was pain here, mainly to do with animals. Dad had shot a cow once, with a .30–06, a powerful hunting rifle displayed in the gun cabinet and never used. We had spent the winter keeping her alive after she breach-birthed a large calf, born dead, which paralyzed her. Dad tried everything: cattle prod (small electric shock), ropes to pull her up, feed left a few feet away. Nothing worked, and by spring she had lost her will. The sight of him pulling the calf from her, then stuffing the bloody womb back inside, stuck with me, later punctuated by the snap of her head at the rifle shot.

Another time we had to trick one of Roy's Holstein milk cows into the trailer so we could take her to the farm. Her name was Blue because her black spots were faded; she was like a family pet and had been raised in the lot behind our house. She trusted us and when the men released her on the farm she bawled and ran, chased by the other cattle who smelled a stranger in their midst. I remember sitting between my brother and Dad as the pickup pulled away. They looked straight ahead, pointed toward their futures; I looked back, silently crying in the cab.

Down in the draw was another scene of pain, also born of love, both intensifying the other. Two days before he died, Dad had been shoring up the eroded banks there with broken concrete and what we called "river rocks." Feeling bad, he went back into town, thinking he had heat exhaustion. Two days later he died instantly of a heart attack while taking a shower. He and Mother were planning a trip, and she had called out to him. No answer. The so-called river I now knew to be part of the Middle Alamosa—those putty-colored rocks a remembrance of eruptions that made the Rocky Mountains and sealed off the plains, creating the Ogallala Aquifer. The seepages of draws. I take these rocks to be a shrine, the last work he did on our place. He was a man of few words, Bob Armitage—quiet, inscrutable. Sometimes he appeared a total mystery. Yet he was a great storyteller and in his own way convivial, certainly well liked and respected. He could tell a story, straight faced, and if it was funny or ironic, could keep that poker face to the very end—even though tears of laughter welled in his eyes, giving him away. My own yearning to communicate with him I connect with that pull I feel beyond the draws to the distant canyons and the Canadian, both seemingly out of reach. Now I know my dad and I had a wordless bond—that of looking caringly at the object of our affections, the land before us. The silence and the space it inhabited was our story. And ours, such a modest place—those draws—our own habit of landscape.

⋁ The plowing made me see time differently: looking back while moving forward. I checked over my shoulder to see if the rows were coming out straight while at the same time I moved ahead through the unplowed ground creating them. These comings and goings connect like the wishbone of draws joined out north. Memory isn't about the past, it's about the process of shaping a continuity. I got off, shimmied down the creek bank, where I parted the barbed wire, and climbed over.

CHAPTER TWO

Springs

I must have been three or so when my brother decided to deposit me in a recently dug posthole. Upright, only the top of my curly brown hair visible, I fit with my arms at my side, inhaling slightly damp earth. It was like being put down, like a mother cow would her baby. I remained still like a small hidden calf. It was only a couple of minutes or so; my brother, in his pranks, was that gentle.

I wondered about this, whether I prompted this memory by looking at a photograph taken at the time, or if I could really still sense that deep hole and surprising calm. Memory is a recalling with invention. Either way, the image of that round head encircled by the hole gave me perspective. I tell myself: when you see yourself as part of a story, then you're really living.

Am I seeking that story this first day as I track the Middle Alamosa, or just seeing where the dried-up creek goes? I think my aim is more to shed the self, to disappear into something larger, to focus outward rather than inward. The land lies before me in a green summer, dotted by cholla past bloom, puckered pink remains tipping the spiked limbs. Yucca are profuse too, their vanilla pods linger, reminding me of the term "Staked Plains" given these expansive prairies—not that their random stands could keep you from getting lost. The sky is of unbelievable blue clarity, moisture in the air, a bank of small clouds rounding the west horizon. I stand at our north fence property line, acutely aware that through the years I have not crossed over—at least not here. Our neighbor, Tom Green, always gave us access. Private land—that's mostly the makeup of Texas; something like the Middle Alamosa landscape remains a secret known only to landowners and friends.

"Shoot yes, Shelley," he said at the post office when I asked. "You know you can come in, drive around, whatever, anytime." I liked Tom's casualness though I knew he was erudite and we might talk as easily about a history he was reading as a recent rain. He appeared indigent—faded overalls, frayed checked shirt—yet he drove a Lincoln Continental. There was an often-told story about Tom going to Amarillo to buy a new car. He showed up at the Cadillac dealership looking like he'd just shipped a load of cattle (which he very well may have). Work shirt torn and worn at the elbows, Levis with holes before this was fashionable, a dirt-rimmed cowboy hat looking like it had barely survived a stampede. The salesmen cut their eyes and seemed to avoid him, like he was a derelict guy just off the streets. After waiting a bit and still no service, Tom crossed the street to the Lincoln dealership and paid cash for a new Continental.

Still it felt strange to climb over that fence—not following designated roads, just wandering.

But the wandering followed the purposeful creek bed. I wanted to sense its story, glimpse its intelligence along the way. Here before me lay the canyons, which had beckoned for a lifetime—a land I had privileged over my own—and now in my slightly arthritic fifties, I parted the fence to engage the mystery, to answer the pull.

I'd been on Green's ranch through the years. Tom and Tommy Lou, his wife, had us out to fish on a small stocked pond and of course to the ranch house and even to his camp for cookouts—a special getaway he had created for himself in a cluster of juniper up a side canyon a considerable distance from the house. As a girl, I was part of a science class whose field trip on the ranch resulted in scouring exposed dinosaur bones on a cliff overlooking what might have been a valley of the Middle Alamosa Creek. We'd found a raccoon den that day too, and were more excited about seeing the babies tucked there than the fossil site. "Don't touch them," our teacher commanded. "Your scent might make the mother reject them when she comes back." Look, don't touch. Given the chance of seeing bobcat, antelope, horned toads, and rattlesnakes, we rightly preferred that dictum to the same order issued for the shiny toys for sale in town.

I ignored all the prohibitions of elementary school this day, with the sun ripe already at 8:30 in the morning (late start) and the mesquite and prickly pear cactus ready to sting you all the way. I wore tennis shoes for comfort (this is snake country) and carried a small backpack with sandwich, water, and camera. The big-brimmed hat was an afterthought that the ever-present Panhandle wind blew off repeatedly. As always, I caught my pants on the parted barbed wire. Hardly the auspicious beginning of a bona fide explorer. I kept thinking of the children's song: "When the Bear comes over the mountain / To see what he could see." Perhaps when you can see your life as a *highly ironic* story is when you really begin to live. My plan: hike as far as you can and check your watch, allowing the same amount of time to return. I did park the white Jeep Comanche pickup on a rise before crossing into Green's. I hoped its reflection would give sign when I returned.

My one preparation had been to check the aerial maps at the Farm Security Administration office. Friends who worked there were happy to turn me loose in the back storage room filled with 1930s black-and-white aerial photographs, each two by two feet square. After wrestling with one or two, trying to get my bearings from the descriptions on each folder, I asked if I could lay them out, thinking I could start at Armitage Farms and follow the Middle Alamosa on the photo maps. I knew the creek would lead me into Tom Green's, but I wasn't sure where it went after that. Fifteen minutes later, I was on hands and knees, putting together each square, like puzzle pieces, of the twenty-something miles to the Canadian. Each square had to be jaggedly matched up, and by now the photos had snaked out of the storage room. Down on all fours, I looked up at the employees at their desks and asked if I could continue across the next room. I was headed for the bathroom. And I was discovering the maps covered the Middle Alamosa Creek and its drainage through the twenty-five thousand acres of Green's Ranch, then the twenty-four thousand acres of Mansfield's Ranch.

When it became evident to all that following the mapped creek to the river would likely put me out the back door and into the Vega Methodist Church parking lot across the street, the agent in the next office offered to make me a topographic map. Sadly I relinquished the original photographic quest, the size and scale so dramatic, thanked him for the rolled up, colorized topo map, and was set for the day.

Maps mess with your mind—or maybe I should say your body.
I wished for Old Father Wind in the map's corner, and maybe a
dragon or two (rattlesnake in this case?) decorating the bottom.
Those images seemed closer to what I was feeling, standing on the
hill above the North Draw, seduced by the prairie ahead, anticipating
the unknowns of plunging canyons and rugged breaks. The FSA
office map, tacked up on my wall in my study, detailed the abrupt
shift from the neat little rectangles of farms to the feathering mass of
canyon lands dominating the upper three-fourths of the county. How
to get one's bearings on the flattened imagery of this map? What of
the older explorer's maps? I made a mental note to try to find those.
Several expeditions had crossed in the mid-1880s; Coronado and
Juan Oñate, in the 1500s and early 1600s; and before that there may
have been "maps" scratched into rock faces, the area frequented by
Paleo-Indian, Archaic, and Historic period peoples. Human occupation dated back to at least 9200 B.P. As if a reminder of that fact, as I
unhooked my snagged Levis from the barbed wire fence, a slender
shard of Tecovas flint appeared in the fencerow below. Surely this
talisman, not the fancy topo map, signified I was on the right trail.
Look, don't touch. I picked it up.

Tecovas is a local "flint"—actually jasper, of reddish purple hue,
captured from the sandstone deposits streaking the nearby canyons.
I instantly felt a connection with someone before me, someone who
knew a thing or two about draws, tributaries, and canyons. No com-
pass, no map, heading now into what my old turtle brain sensed was
north; I was vulnerable. But "lonely" was not something I ever felt
among the population of rocks, grasses, critters, and flint shards.

Having read translations of the Spanish chroniclers and the
reports of U.S. government explorers, I wanted their vision at first,
seeing vastness only, details overwhelmed. I could sense the curve
of the earth, so pervasive in this horizontal view—earth and sky,
earth and sky. I've had that feeling driving west into Vega from
Amarillo as the road lifts slightly, realizing its four-thousand-foot
elevation. And at the farm, driving there, when something appears
on the far horizon, then disappears (a plow, corrals), it's a sure sign
of elevation change but so slight, as the road seems level. When Col.
Charles Goodnight first rode along the seemingly endless plains to

First hike into the canyons on Green's Ranch. *Author photo.*

the abrupt thousand-foot drop of nearby Palo Duro Canyon, he was surprised and awed despite previous reports of its existence. As I walked toward the ground's slightest darkening ahead, I understood the genius of the Comanche and Kiowa who eluded the U.S. Calvary repeatedly by disappearing into the landscape.

Here now: the first canyon. Purposely, I started here on top, rather than from the North Draw that ran into Green's. I wanted to descend into the canyon, connect that way to the Middle Alamosa. I leaned over the lip and looked maybe three hundred feet straight down. A caliche-lined edge scalloped the rim, cascading walls shining pale orange, cream, and reddish brown. The shale and sandstone looked fragile and there were eroded holes on top where you could see through to the canyon bottom. What surprised me was the height and density of mostly deciduous trees there. If this is only a side canyon of the Middle Alamosa, still water seeps and runs. Though the day is mostly calm—one of those rare days the wind averages less than sixteen miles per hour—the color, shape, texture, and attitude of the rocks signal the movement of wind, water, gravity.

Now how to get down?

Even our lapsed animal selves can detect lateral movement, the hairs rising on our necks when a shadow passes. I saw something

A mule deer leads the way into the canyon. *Author photo.*

large move along a slope about two hundred yards away. Quietly, I eased the pack off, got the camera, and used the zoom lens as binoculars. I saw a mule deer carefully edging his way down the cliff-side, grazing occasional forbs among the rocks. He had not seen or smelled me so I had the luxury of watching his nimble descent. This, my second talisman of the day and my guide into the canyon.

I waited until he was out of sight and then began to follow him in my not-so-graceful climb down. About halfway, the gravelly edge turned to a grassy bunker; he had found the gentlest slope, the easiest way. The lushness of the canyon bottom surprised me again. Here the trees—locust and a few young cottonwoods—offered shade and some of their green secret: a tiny strand of water meandered through the soft red clay. The Middle Alamosa must have its own fingerlings of moisture. This was run-off from a wet summer. Or was it a creek bed?

Could there even be springs nearby?

The maps trisected my thoughts. "Middle Alamosa" appeared on the soil map, starting from the highway runoff into the draw at the farm's South Place. On another map, the name appeared just north-east over on Kim Montgomery's across the county road. Same draw, farther down. For years I had witnessed occasional high rises—the result of intense rain storms that flooded the draw, fence post to fence post, streaming over the county road, sounding like a rushing stream until the water washed by. High rises were few but memorable, water backed up to the highway, dangerous to cross until the rush was sated. I lingered in the canyon, listening. But surely more than occasional cloudbursts must feed the tributary.

The topo map showed the myriad canyons to be veins, like those on a leaf or like hands spread wide, veins blue with life as the map indicated elevation and flora by color. There were apparently dozens of these deep cuts, some registering darker on the map, for depth. A blue dot midway on the highway draw indicated Dad's tank where the catfish had hidden out; down draw on Kim's place was a blue splayed area, maybe another dam. Water seemed a clue to how the canyons connected, how the entire landscape was on its way to the river. I followed the trickle down the canyon.

Sometimes the water disappeared into the red mud and choking grasses, coursing into another ecosystem—scrub locust, shin oat, sprigs of cottonwood. Around a jagged wall, I discovered a pooling of water, which of course I hoped was spring fed, but it appeared stagnant, probably a "plunge pool," a water catcher from the cliffs above. Algae eddied in the slight wind. A dead monarch floated upon the milky green, an early presence, August its usual time of migration. Again, a shadow passed over me, made me look up. The camera zoom served once more as binoculars, and I spotted a great horned owl reeling away, up canyon. He disappeared in the buff-colored boulders above, wonderfully camouflaged. His B-52 body reminded me that he too might serve as talisman, or maybe an avatar for our age.

I was out eight hours that day and lost the whole time. The water and sandwich were meted out at the locked green gate where I turned around. Flint in the roadway thrilled me, the Tecovas reds but also the multicolored and striated Alibates mined from a dolomite quarry northeast of Amarillo. The canyon had led to another and another, the trickle of water long gone but my fascination continuing the flow. I passed a cabin, one of maybe three habitations between our farm and the Canadian River, later realizing it was Tom Green's camp (I had reached it before on a road on the other side). Somehow I had strayed away from the Middle Alamosa and the wishbone draws.

I talked to myself. Even though I chose to go alone, to experience this first day without human voices, I enjoyed my own. But still, I was shocked when it broke the silence. I laughed at how companioned I was. I spoke to hawks overhead, a tiny frog fruit forb below. *Hello. Hello.* Even though I talked out loud, mostly the day filled me with fresh sensations; I felt wonderfully emptied of what one of my college professors had dubbed "syphillization."

Several times I climbed out of the canyons to get my bearings. On the way back my talisman deserted me as I headed in the opposite direction. I lost concentration and shimmied down sloping shale walls without a thought for rattlesnakes in the tufts of brush I grabbed all around. There were rustlings; I ignored them. Finally I recognized the first canyon where I'd been heisted. Somehow I had returned on the opposite side, but the reflection of the north windmill blades caught my eye in the distance. Across was the North Draw; and there on the hill, the pickup. What I thought about was the land in terms of water—its delicate fickleness, its presence marked by the layered walls even in its absence. How it had marked the maps, a language of echoes.

⩔ Back in Vega, I asked Tom Henry, Tom's son, about the springs.

"Oh, yeah. The Middle Alamosa is bullshit," he mouthed over the rattles of idling diesel trucks, leaning out of the cab of his pickup at the local Allsup's. It was past ten at night and Tom Henry obviously had been at an earlier watering hole. Hoping not to appear a complete fool, I described my first hike and the questions I had about water.

"Sure, I remember when I was a kid there were lots of springs. But now, shit, there may be only two."

Where are they, I wanted to ask, but didn't. Why was I always so shy? I remembered a time out at Tom Henry's place when a group of us were trying to get directions to Little Arrowhead, an archaeological site of the late archaic Antelope Creek Phase people. We had a topo map spread out on the hood of the pickup. Tom Henry dismissed it with a flourish of his thick, ranch-worn hands. I can see the glint of his wedding band flashing on a swollen finger as he gestured. "Just go over that hill," he pointed, "bear left. You'll see a road that takes you right to the place. Can't miss it." He repeated this last missive several times. We missed it—not altogether because of his directions. But still, a sweep of the hand toward the horizon seemed like a slight of hand to us neophytes.

There *were* springs, though. He had said it. I thought about a crossing you take on the next ranch north of his toward the river. Mansfield's. It was at the bottom of a hill, always green with brush, cattails, hackberry, and salt cedar, cattle usually muddying the slew. I doubted the water survived from only runoff. Our area is categorized as semidesert. Despite the established average precipitation of twenty inches a year, evaporation claims most of that, and we never make the twenty inches anymore. The closer to the river you get, the more porous and absorbing the red clay soils. The crossing was over Ranch Creek, another "intermittent" stream.

My plan had been to follow the draws into the supposedly continuous "canyon" of the Middle Alamosa Creek. At first, I wanted to hike by myself all the way. I saw myself walking, camping, supplies dropped by friends along the way. But this was not simple; for one thing ranch roads didn't necessarily reach the Middle Alamosa. And now, after the first challenge of reading the canyons—which was a main canyon? which a feeder?—I realized I needed help. Tom Henry's kind of help was one thing. Research, study, involving others was another. The project conceived so simply suddenly took on a serpentine life, not unlike the landscape.

How did it happen? I don't remember. But I was at Roark's Hardware in Vega when I mentioned the Middle Alamosa to Randy Roark. Randy is fifteen years younger; I didn't know him in school but knew the family. His mother and father had been family friends: Shirley briefly my first grade teacher (until she got pregnant and had to resign) and Bud a long-time businessman running the family hardware. Like the drugstore, the hardware store was essential to small-town farming and ranching life. I still liked going there, remembering the old nail bins and lines of shelves where I played hide and seek while my dad picked up hard-to- find bolts and such for the farm tractor.

Randy has kept the store the same—adding to the walls full of antique scythes, wagon wheels, old implements, deer heads, and photos of the registered paint horses Bud raised. There's the Vega

Drugstore counter—once home to the best sodas in three counties. It's now the counter for ordering and billing. There's Ed's old printing press. There's the old popcorn machine, still five cents a bag. Peanut shells crunch under your shoes; locals sip coffee, crack the nuts, play with the current hardware cat. Lots of stories get swapped here along with bits, combine parts, bridles.

"I deliver our mineral mix in the blue tubs—you've probably seen them out there—every few days to Green's and Mansfield's," he said after admitting he had never heard of the Middle Alamosa. "I drive out there all the time. We should go some time. Let's go find those springs."

"Some time" quickly became "this Sunday" (and many other Sundays), and with a stash of water bottles, cheese, and crackers (my modest contribution), we mounted his Ford 150 four-wheel drive and headed out. This was pure luxury compared to my small Jeep pickup, clutch smoking when I ground up and down the hills.

At first I felt I was cheating. My original plan had been to follow the landscape, the whims of water and wind, only on foot. But now I told myself a measure of reconnaissance was needed. I would locate certain sites—like the springs—then hike back to them and from them to the next site. I would cover all the Middle Alamosa on foot, but use the truck to establish the segments of the thirty miles. I wanted the puzzle and the connections too.

That's the idea Randy had the first day—to reconnoiter. I thought we were going out to Green's; he pulled off Highway 385 early. We were headed into Kim Montgomery's.

"You mentioned springs and I remembered when we were kids we came down here to the old picnic grounds—that's what people called them—you remember? We boys came down here, somewhere around here, and skinny-dipped in a big lake that must have been fed by springs."

I resisted imagining Randy's naked, lean body gleaming in the water. It was easier if in my mind he stayed just a kid with a bunch of other boys.

The idea that so much water could be here in these arid hills shocked me. It seemed geographically impossible. And that it was on my neighbor's land, in the same draw (the Middle Alamosa Creek) that passed from our land into his! I had stood along that fence many times on our

South Place, sensing the artificiality of private ownership and property lines, seeking connections, not divisions, looking up the draw.

But I didn't believe it.

Randy made me a little nervous. He was handsome, slim, six feet tall, that male model look with the day-old stubble dramatizing the sharp jaw. What was a good-looking "available" younger man doing with me, middle-aged salt and pepper me? What had I heard—that he was divorced? That he was gay? You could hear anything in a small town, and I was especially glad I couldn't hear what people might say about of me. *Independent, she never married, did she, comes back to that family farmhouse alone in the summers, heard she has someone special in New Mexico, or did I see a car there? No children!!!* Tsk. Tsk.

We parked on a hill overlooking what had to be a very wide and deep cut—an enormous "creek" bed, dry of course. In the bottom were a blue couch and a grill. Randy explained that Kim liked to bring his family out here for cookouts. Of course. I remembered the place now. We had come here on school hayrides, thrown from one side of the tractor-pulled trailer to the other, riding the haystacks, hoping to be rocked into the arms of our current teenage heartbeat.

I had ridden the haystack with tremulous romance in my veins. Randy had gone skinny-dipping.

The July afternoon was long and hot. Oftentimes the creek cut we followed was so deep the banks were above our heads. Along the banks were grapevines, and the bottom was strewn with protruding tree branches and tripping roots. We stumbled on. Another owl flew by. When we could see out of the banks there were fields of sunflowers or large patches of Russian thistle. The diversity and size of trees and brush and the slightly wet creek bottom spelled water. But we couldn't find any.

Then, after Randy had apologized for at least the fifth time for taking us on a wild goose chase, we rounded a bend in the creek, and there in the distance was a lake, ringed in thick weeds, maybe a football field in size. We circled part of it, but both of us knew we sought the source. Hiking over the dam to a pool of clearer water—striders on top, the bottom visible—we worked our way back to a stand of partially dead cottonwoods, some nearly fifty feet tall. The canopy

Springs site on Montgomery's Ranch. *Author photo.*

shifted. The trees were studded with hulking night herons. A couple of great blue herons laboriously took off. This must be a rookery. But only if there is consistent water.

We never found the exact seep that day. The brush was too thick. But the eddying of the pond near the back of the narrowing canyon indicated a spring. We stood as if admiring a fine monument, a somber yet hopeful event. It was like witnessing a miracle. Quiet was what Randy and I shared, and some fond ribbing. There was easy talk in the cab, but when we hiked and looked and listened ours was a companionable solitude. I sensed his boredom at the store and with Vega (he had originally left the small town, lived in Sedona, Arizona, played on the mixed pro volleyball circuit, hooking up with some Brazilian woman for a while). I was never bored, seeing the Middle Alamosa project expand like the frond-shaped canyons on my topo map back home.

And so the hikes continued. Solo hikes, hikes with friends. Hikes linking together the winding, looping, and disappearing sections of the Middle Alamosa. And the research: geology, geography, archaeology, history; interviews with locals and academic experts. I liked to spend the day out, or a morning or evening if I could only spare it, come home and research, make notes, print and sort photographs. I had traveled abroad this way and now it was my own backyard. Next trip out along the Middle Alamosa, I took the canyon just below the spring-fed lake into Green's, and this time found myself on the east side of Tom's camp walking the Middle Alamosa. Here the creek was wide—approximately forty feet in places—and red. Water was here now; the drama of the soil's change from the farm to here showed as brownish or sand-colored water become a reddish orange as you entered the Permian layers. I laughed to myself as I recalled a scene with Don Taylor, a childhood playmate who was with my family on vacation at Carlsbad Caverns. We kids bugged the portly park ranger with our endless questions. After we asked one way or another what made these underground enormous caverns, he shrugged, "Ground water. Just ground water."

The tributary color is a clue to the name of the river it serves. Today in New Mexico some old timers still call the river the Colorado, red river. So why "Canadian"—a strange name, people say, for a Texas river.

I'd read that the presence of Spanish explorers inspired the name of this watercourse, defined by breaks, or *cañones*. Some researchers believed the river got its name from French Canadian fur trappers who briefly entered the area. By 1845 Lt. James W. Abert, conducting a reconnaissance expedition down the river's course through New Mexico and the Texas Panhandle, declared the river's name came from "the great cañon through which it flows." Yet the earlier Stephen Harriman Long expedition of 1820 recorded no explanation for the name already in common usage. I learned that historian Beryl Roper, in her "How Did This River Come to Be Called Canadian," contended that "Canadian" may have issued from various printings and translations in which the Spanish tilde was dropped or omitted.

It's true that English-trained ears (and tongues) easily grafted and altered Spanish names. For example, the Spanish *la reata* became lariat; *lazo*, lasso; and *botas*, boots. Once when Randy and I sought a creek named on the map Sierrita de la Cruz (already corrupted from the Spanish *cerrita*, or "little hill" to "little mountain"), we asked a local cowboy for help. "Never heard of it," he said at first. Then he removed his hat, scratched his head and pondered: "Do you mean 'Sweetly Cruise?'"

Canadian River in west Oldham County. *Author photo.*

As for "Middle Alamosa," the original designation on older maps is "Alamosa," though two other large tributaries join it, one on the east and the other on the west, before it empties into the Canadian. Spanish language place names mostly stop at Amarillo, thirty-five miles east of Vega, suggesting the range of Spanish and later hispanos into the area from the west. Whether entering the Panhandle from west or east, the subsequent American explorers found a well-developed trail through the sea of grass before them, and this trail followed the water sources, the playa lakes, the Canadian River—and the springs.

I began to see the pattern of water in the breaks as a series of nexus points. Power points if you will. The Middle Alamosa Creek, or MAC as I started to call it, ran south to north; people had appeared to cross from east to west and west to east by skirting the *barrancas*, as Coronado's generation called the breaks, for the more easily navigated flatlands. At these crossings, the axis of tributary and trail, were water sources, oftentimes springs. Traveling the Middle Alamosa became a matter of recognizing these hubs of energy and survival and the tributary's function in the larger region.

⋁ We could barely make out the crown of Randy's western straw hat from the flat gray sandstone slab where Lisa and I stood. Lisa Jackson, an archaeological assistant from the Panhandle-Plains Historical Museum in nearby Canyon, Texas, had been here before with archaeology club members, so she jumped at the chance to ride with Randy and me to this site. With her dark almond eyes and straight black hair, Lisa could pass for an ancestral guide, except for her load of archaeological gear: snake shin protectors, fanny pack with two water bottles, vest with multiple pockets, GPS tracker, and safari hat.

"What's down there, Randy?" I yelled, thinking he couldn't hear from inside the cavern he had just slipped into.

"Bunch of daddy longlegs spiders marching all around." Lisa and I wrinkled our noses and were silently glad he wanted to climb into the cistern first.

Lisa gave us some history. "Last time we were here, one of the older members of the society fell in one of these and there was a rattle-snake in the bottom. Dead though." The guy was rescued, pulled out, hustled back to Amarillo in shock. They worried he might have had a heart attack. Bad luck. But I was fixated on Randy's bobbing head and what he said:

"Lots of pictographs . . ."

"Petroglyphs," Lisa corrected.

"Well, rock art, whatever. Medicine men, I think."

"Shamans," Lisa echoed.

We leaned over to look. Squinting this way and that, dodging the whiteout of the noonday sun, we could barely make out large figures etched in the walls of the circular underground cone. The shamans had diamond-shaped bodies; some had sparkler-like fingers, as if to exude power. There were several of these cisterns, or "solution cavi-ties," as Lisa noted they were called. We first thought of them solely as water catchers. Despite her training, Lisa was fond of saying no one knew for sure. But Randy and I liked to surmise. This was a place of water, a place of shamans. This was a sacred place.

Adjacent to the solution cavities, a banking, red sandstone ledge sheltered the nearby springs. The water was colored an orangey-red by the clay, but we could see a tiny, clear seepage from clustered pebbles

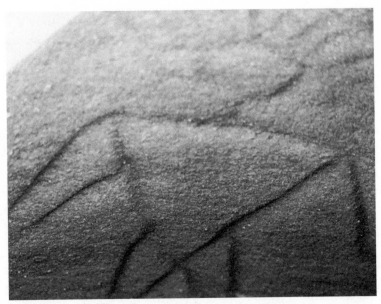

Shaman petroglyph at the Bison Run. *Author photo.*

underneath the overhang. We had pitched down into this gulley without a clue to the water's existence. The drive here was relatively flat and featureless—the expected grass, red earth, sagebrush plain. Then suddenly a small arroyo, and to the east the outcropping and sandstone slabs. Even with Randy's former instructions and Lisa's previous knowledge, we had nearly missed it. In this country you needed a spatial sense beyond word of mouth.

The site, popularly called the Bison Run, is on private ranch property west of Vega and Adrian, off the *ceja*, or brow, of the caprock. But mercifully it's not popularly known and is not accessible for most. Archaeologists and ranchers both try to keep such locations a secret. Vandalism and pot hunting has been a long-standing problem in Oldham County.

The bison knew where it was. Lisa led us to what continued to amaze all who visited. I had to be hassled to leave the fixating shamans and surprising springs. I trailed along behind.

Across the creek bed that veered off from the spring, through bunkers of tumbleweeds and scratchy sage, stood several red sandstone

Bison Run petroglyph. *Author photo.*

boulders. On one of them, probably a surface of five square feet or
so, was the namesake of the place. A large bison petroglyph covered
the boulder in a style that suggested prehistoric imagery. Below it, an
image that looked at first like a handprint, then a rattle. It could also
be a pointer, an indicator of what we saw next, east of it: the bison trail.

The trail's depth—at least a foot deep into hard sandstone—says
it all. For "no one knows for sure" how many years, bison frequented
this springs, as did the American Indians whose petroglyphs remain.
We call them "buffalo." I learned that bison, known as *Bison bison*,
made two kinds of trails. The western writer Mari Sandoz mentioned
feeder trails worn by bison in search of both pasture and water.
These trails were seasonally used, approximately twelve inches wide
to allow the single passage of small hooves. Some slopes might have
as many as fifty such trails running alongside one another. But as I
examined this trail—lightly stepping into it as if the ground might
still echo a shaggy presence—I found it resembled more closely the
description of Martin S. Garretson, writing for the American Bison
Society. He explains that deeper trails, like this one etched and

smoothed by years of use, were migratory, often running north and south as the bison sought suitable weather and fodder. Wasn't that what I had read about what is now Highway 385 from Tascosa south to Hereford, Texas? Yes, our own highway was once a migratory bison trail, running from present day Boys' Ranch, site of Old Tascosa, first established at Atascosa Creek and its springs, through Vega in southern Oldham County, then south, where it crossed Tierra Blanca Creek, near another springs east of Hereford, Texas.

Stunned by the beauty of the pure line of the petroglyph, none of us thought to measure the glass-smooth hard-wrought trail. And just when Randy and I began to search the brush for more, possibly overgrown, trails, we heard a loud pop and a cry behind us. Lisa had started back to the truck for water but stumbled crossing the rise from the springs. She was on the ground and obviously in pain. At first I thought snakebite, but when we got there her ankle was already swelling. Laid up for the day, she insisted on riding the rest of the time in the back seat of the extended cab, her leg elevated on the ice cooler, and her ankle packed in ice. Later x-rays showed a broken ankle. Bad luck. We joked that the shaman didn't approve of our snooping. No matter what might be measured and named, we were humbled before the secrets of the place that were sure to remain a mystery.

I thought about the time in Vega I encountered Calvin Peters, then manager of Fulton's Ranch north of town and once a heavy-footed rebounder for the Adrian High School basketball team who fogged dirt from the ceilings of the gym each time he hit the floor with a ball. Decked out in his cowboy best—blood- and manure-stained boots, worn Levis tucked into them, chaps flapping in the wind, a faded bandana around his neck, and yes, the well-trodden cowboy hat—he was standing in the driveway of Groneman's service station when I pulled up. Nearby was his rig, a hefty four-wheel drive outfit with a double trailer on back. He appeared to be looking for something, so I pulled up and joked out the window, "Are you lost, Calvin?" A character, Calvin gave me a droll look. "Nope. I'm looking for buffalo." I expected anything but this retort, so I just looked at him.

"Yeah, Fulton's buffalos have wandered down this direction and I thought I'd better gather them before some tourist gets hurt." I liked it when the guys came in from working on the ranches because they gave a serious nudge to the Hollywood sheen of the celluloid heroes. I'd seen some tourists slow down and stare, particularly when a couple of the guys pulled up to the Dairy Queen drive-in window on their horses.

Buffaloes in Vega, all the way from Fulton's Ranch? Maybe the migratory instinct was still there.

Tourists and Vega people alike tend to think of Route 66 as the main historical claim of the county. Bill Russell, a local amateur historian and devoted Canadian Breaks sleuth, told me about a time he and our sheriff, David Medlin, were checking out old trails and settlements in the western part of the county, along Trujillo Creek. They topped a ridge, thinking mostly of history past, and saw down below, bedded down in high valley grass, a buffalo. They were as amazed as if they had seen the mythical white buffalo of Indian lore. Bill said when he reported this to the local coffee drinkers they barely nodded, persisting in their tales of Route 66. Some said they didn't even believe buffalo had ever roamed these plains in great numbers—and they had no notion of the almost incomprehensible extermination, estimated at forty million total in the Great Plains. These southern plains were the last stand of the buffalo after 1871, when the north plains were cleared. The grasses along the Canadian valleys south and west of Tascosa were favorite feeding grounds. These herds, described by observers as so numerous that they looked like a black storm on the horizon and, according to one horseman, stretched across the entire Panhandle as he rode, were also the last to give sustenance to the Comanche and Kiowa. Bill said the conversation stopped when one of the coffee drinkers offered that he had actually found buffalo horns on his place.

Bill and David might have been close to Blue Goose Springs on Trujillo Creek. Here, thronged by cottonwood—habitat for varieties of hawks, the yellow flash of warblers and orioles—the springs seep from sandstone. Most of Oldham County's springs flow from Ogallala sand and caliche, Triassic sandstone, and a few from Permian dolomite. Researcher Gunnar M. Brune, author of *Springs of Texas*, an invaluable volume that set the standard for investigation of this little-studied, little-regulated resource, claimed that Oldham County once had a wealth of springs, chiefly because of great differences in land elevation near the Canadian River. But he cautioned in his 1980s research that he found the springs much less numerous and copious than they had been under virgin conditions. Primarily the decline of the Ogallala Aquifer at the time was due to irrigation, population explosion, and cycles of drought. What would he say today?

At Paint Rock, known in the expeditionary annals as Rocky Dell, the causes seem almost attitudinal. Located about thirteen miles west of Vega on another tributary of the Canadian, Agua Piedras Creek, Paint Rock was a favorite destination of area residents until the current owner started denying access. Randy and I were able to get permission to visit, and when we arrived we could see why people weren't allowed in anymore.

Years of signatures and drawings were scratched in the rock, beneath the sandstone overhang that makes the site so dramatic. Several members of the Ivy family, early owners of the ranch, had inscribed their names or signatures, along with countless recreationalists from Vega and Adrian. Back under, on the gray sandstone wall, are pictographs, colored red, ochre, blue—mostly faded or compromised in some way. The site is badly damaged from use: by picnickers, skinny-dippers, even someone who chalked over the drawings, perhaps to make them stand out better in a photograph. Standing before these images—of historical and perhaps prehistorical lineage—you're struck by the persistence of pure pigment. Like a badly abused painting that has been painted over or poorly repaired, here the canvas is cracked (ledges fallen), the foreground destroyed (recent footprints obliterating pictograph footprints). I look up and see fragile, faint images, seemingly in flight. Here, what appears to be a blue angel (another shaman?), and there, what may be a dog, a longhorn. Each is a possible clue to the age of the pictographs. The dog—if indeed it is a dog—could suggest knowledge of earlier occupants: the Apache-like Jumados who used dog travois and displaced the earlier Antelope Creek Phase peoples.

The images tell the tale of continuous visitation and gathering. I imagine Lt. W. R. Whipple, surveying a route for a railroad from the Mississippi River to the Pacific for the War Department in 1853, standing on the lip of the Paint Rock cavern. In his record of that day—one in which he and his men, like the American Indian and Comanchero traders before him, enjoyed a "stream" that flowed through the gorge and that, as he described it, ran along "a shelving sandstone rock form[ing] a sort of cave"—he attempted to sketch the pictographs. His stick figure–like renderings must have been comical to visiting Pueblo Indians, especially compared to the colorful pictographs. Remarkably Whipple communicated with these visitors from the West, who confirmed that this had been a favorite buffalo range where their people hunted, feasted, and danced—recording their deeds on the stone. They explained that the most dramatic of the pictographs, the Awanyu, Plumed Serpent—the purplish-blue ten-foot-long undulation that today most captivates us—was inspired by the power of Montezuma. It is a great water snake, a bringer of rain and preserver of those who would pray to him. Among other paintings, the "horned" men they explained as buffalo dancers.

Buffalo and water.

Randy and I crossed the now dry creek bed and just as we suspected, on the ledge adjacent to the cave work several deep buffalo trails convened. Here were grinding holes, so well used their circular interiors caked yellow in a rind of plant preparation. We wondered what pollen dating might reveal about the nature and age of the procured plants. From across the way we could imagine the earlier "commerce of the prairies," as Josiah Gregg, another Panhandle explorer, called it. Comancheros—Mexican traders with the Comanche—had met Comanche, Kiowa, and Pueblo people here, all bartering for horses in exchange for guns, whiskey, slaves, trinkets. Perhaps we were being too hard on the locals, thinking of them as the only partiers.

But unlike the Bison Run, this place had been abandoned by the gods. Or so Randy and I sensed. The springs, spent; the energy of such a ceremonial place, deadened by the later din of careless campers. We walked, saddened—peering at the marred images, hoping that by holding them in our hearts they would stay a little longer. Randy spotted another date, 1810. Yes, the southern route of the Santa Fe Trail ran just a mile and a quarter south of here.

We saw something else, something that defied the deadening we felt. An elliptical mass of tree branches, like horns locked together, taller than Randy, lay balanced on the ledge just down from the rock art. At first I thought it was something washed up from the creek, something like organized debris, but that didn't make sense.

And then of course we realized it was the nest of an eagle, possibly a golden eagle, largest raptor in our area. Where had it come from? We scoured the top of the cliff but saw no trees in the parched place. It seemed to have dropped from the sky. We measured ourselves by it. We came up short. The magnitude and perfection of this nesting made us look further up the blemished creek. If there was life, then where was the source? And then we saw it, about a hundred yards from the site, a green area—a seeps still flowing.

Ⅴ We couldn't begin to measure the health of these springs, but we found their existence in this arid land, which in our lifetimes was marked by drought more than anything else, something like hope. The most recent scientific documentation of springs by Brune in Oldham County took into account things like latitude, longitude, composition of the water (for example, percentage of dissolved solids, etc.). By these standards, historically Oldham County springs had been healthy and plentiful compared to those of other Panhandle counties. West of Paint Rock and the fragile movement of mosses that had so excited Randy and me is Chavez Springs, noted by Brune as the largest surviving springs in the county. Like many area springs, it flows from the fissures in a collapse zone of Permian beds. Today Chavez Springs plunges over a waterfall, with maidenhair ferns skirting a pool of frogs and fish. Nearby large cottonwoods, elm, and willow bank the creek. The dark gray soils upstream indicate that a bog once extended a least a kilometer more beyond the pool. The day we were there, Randy hugged one of the cottonwoods, his arms reaching around only about an eighth of its circumference.

I discovered a record from the Juan Oñate expedition of 1601, when he and his seventy men camped along these springs. For over four hundred years these springs have flowed, and who knows how much longer? Like us, Oñate was surprised too. As Herbert Eugene Bolton translates Oñate's observations in his *Spanish Explorations:* "Although we feared the lack of watering places for the cattle, there are so many in this country that throughout the journey at distances of three or four leagues there was always sufficient water . . . and in many places there were springs of very good water and groves of trees."

Randy Roark among the cottonwoods, Chavez Springs.
Author photo.

I remembered the grapevines too. Always a sign of sufficient water. On my trips to Paint Rock as a little girl, our friends, then owners of the land, called their ranch "Grapevine." Now I made the connection. In 1845, Lt. James W. Abert, essentially following Oñates's route, commented on "the luxuriant profusion of plum trees and grape vines," implying the fresh water of springs. Other expeditions—those of Whipple and Randolph Marcy—had steered by the springs and playa sites. The bedrock mortars, rock paintings, and other artifacts revealed that prehistoric and historic peoples were led by the springs too. Marcy traveled with an Indian guide to ensure that the settlers he led to California would have sufficient food, fuel, and water. We kids—who took to the dirt and gravel of drying creek beds and banks on places like Ivy's Grapevine ranch and the old picnic grounds near Montgomery's springs, digging with cast-off tablespoons like little archaeologists—had no clue that an oasis that had sustained people and critters for hundreds of years was nearby, slipping like a green water snake through the arid landscape.

⩔ The tributaries, their springs and canyons, and the river itself began to take on epic proportions in my mind. Without the springs there would be no tributaries, no canyons. In a plateau country, rivers and tributaries, all begun by or supplied by springs, have cut the canyons, arroyos, mesas, and draws. The variance of these, their shapes, depend in part on soil differences. In a plateau country like the llano, rainfall and underground water, like springs, may run along hard, nonporous caliche surfaces and cut into softer clays. Elevation speeds the incisions, and the canyons, mesas, and draws wear according to these combinations. So not only are the springs a hub of travel, migration, and settlement, but they help build the highways that connect them. No wonder the Comanche, calling the North Canadian "Wolf River," also described it as a northern boundary of Comancheria. Such mapping designated not a single trail or spring or tributary but a living, changing network of movement.

The Comanche, as linguists are steadily rediscovering, have a particularly "spatial" language suited to this landscape they inhabited. Daniel Gelo, an anthropology professor and researcher specializing in the Comanche, explains this language in his translation and editing of Manuel García Rejón's *Comanche Vocabulary*. For example, the Comanche terms for "distance" allow for three relative grades, a kind of precision that also applies to geographic features such as elevation, vegetation, and bodies of water. And a single word can describe a lake or pond from rainwater (such as a playa), a spring, an abandoned spring, a swampy valley, clear water running, water impoundment, a stream bank, a river channel, and so on. A word can also convey connections or relationship; for non-Comanche speakers such words can function somewhat like metaphors, which link the supposedly unlike together.

Gelo describes these metaphorical indicators as what we might think of as ecological relationships, based, however, not only on the Comanche's botanical knowledge (they identified at least sixty-seven medicinal and food plants, some differentiated down to the level of subspecies) but also on what Gelo calls an energy flow between living things. In his study of Comanche worldview, based on their language, Gelo calls such a "philosophy" a kinship of "sacred motion." For example, they used the same word—*sahtotzip*—to designate both flowers as a category and foam on water; whirlwinds and butterflies carry the same prefix: *uye*. I begin to see the plunge pool on Green's ranch differently: the water foamed by algae and water spiders, the dead monarch butterfly. Still day; stagnant pond. Kinship.

⋁ The vast Ogallala Aquifer, lying underneath portions of eight Great Plains states, including the Panhandle of Texas, is one of the world's largest aquifers, and covers an area of approximately 174,000 miles. When you walk the Middle Alamosa you pass over what modern people believed to be an inexhaustible underground river. The formation of the aquifer dates from the late Miocene to the early Pliocene, some two to six million years ago, when the southern Rocky Mountains were tectonically active. Rivers and streams cut channels generally east or southeast, providing alluvial and aeolian sediment that filled the channels and eventually created the capture of the water-bearing Ogallala Formation. Rivers such as the Brazos in Texas once ran all the way from the Sangre de Cristo Mountains in New Mexico to the Gulf of Mexico before the Pecos River, passing more north and south, "stole" these waters. The Ogallala is deepest when it fills the ancient channels, ranging in thickness from a few feet to one thousand feet in depth. You can imagine an inverted mountain range below now filled with water, the water capped by course sedimentary rocks or, nearer the surface, finer-grained material. Springs issue from water below the surface, from as deep as four hundred feet in the north of the aquifer to one to two hundred feet in the south.

Windmills, invented in the mid-1880s, began the "mining" of prehistoric waters. Irrigation wells first tapped the source in 1911, gaining large-scale use from the Dust Bowl of the 1930s through the 1950s. Affordable technology after World War II led to a water

extraction rate that made the High Plains one of the most agricul-
turally productive regions in the world. Today about 27 percent of
irrigated land in the United States overlies this aquifer, providing
drinking water to approximately 82 percent of the people living
within its boundary. Not surprisingly, some estimates project the
aquifer will be dry by 2030.

There are many causes of this "dewatering." The rate of recharge,
or water entering the aquifer, is limited. Evaporation of surface
waters, the impermeable caliche layer in some areas, and the
destruction of the playas by farmers—along with unbridled irrigation—ensure depletion. The relentless plumbing of the Ogallala
waters—without the benefit of recharge—means we take from a finite
prehistoric source. The steadily falling water table may be read in the
disappearing springs—the "intermittent" creeks.

Paul Horgan, a student of the Pueblo Indians and the New Mexico
landscape, writes in *The Great River* of the power of water realistically
and in the Pueblo imagination. "Gods and heroes were born out of
springs, and ever afterward came and went between the above and
below worlds through their pools. Every pueblo had sacred springs
somewhere nearby. There was every reason to sanctify them—physical,
as life depended upon water; spiritual, as they had natural mystery
which suggested supernatural qualities; for how could it be that when
water fell as rain, or as snow, and ran away, or dried up, there should
be other water which came and came, secretly and sweetly, out of the
ground and never failed."

⋁ Back at the farm, I head up the North Draw, thinking of the next
hike. Sam pulls up behind me.

"Hey, guess what I saw out here the other day?" Another great Sam
story. I lean against the pickup door to hear.

"Big eagle. Maybe a golden, but could have been an immature bald
eagle. Landed up on the windmill."

"Out here? But aren't the bald eagles fond of fish? Don't they usually
hang around water?"

He shrugged.

And then I remembered that over the hill, just up the next draw,
was Kim's springs. Less than a mile away. Well, not really Kim's. A

nameless springs and yet known through time. I'd head on up to the windmill, get a drink of water, that cold well water. Water from the Ogallala, paleowater, dating back to the Ice Age or earlier. Such sweet, fragile kinship, this ancient water.

I opened my mouth to explain to Sam. He'd already started up to check his cattle.

But I wasn't just talking to myself.

CHAPTER THREE

Refuge

No matter how salubrious the Spanish accounts of lush grape vines and plum thickets along the Canadian tributaries, the Anglo explorers who followed later in the nineteenth century thought otherwise. Locations that drew vinicultural praise—one Spanish account recommends a plains variety comparable to grapes used to make a fine Spanish wine—garnered this description from the Long expedition of 1820 as recorded by Edwin James in his *Expedition from Pittsburg to the Rocky Mountains:* "In regard to this extensive section of the country, I do not hesitate in giving the opinion, that it is almost wholly unfit for civilization, and of course uninhabitable by a people depending on agriculture for their subsistence. Although tracks of fertile land considerably extensive are occasionally to be met with, yet the scarcity of wood and water, almost uniformly prevalent, will prove an insuperable obstacle in the way of settling the country." In other words, what would later become Oldham County, Texas—and what for earlier pre-Columbian times had been home to native peoples—was part of the Great American Desert.

Mother and Daddy had sometimes heard this epithet, delivered as a joke, when they traveled to bankers' conventions in places like Kansas City and New Orleans. People from other plains states used it in one-upmanship (my plains are better than yours), and certainly those living on the banks of Lake Pontchartrain in Louisiana had a point. Now I felt like one of those disparaging explorers but in the outland of independent living facilities. Mother had gone from falling in her home to a shaky use of a walker, and falls even with that. As I hiked and researched and photographed in the summers, sharing the adventures with her, we both faced the new territory of moving her from the family home place.

⋎ Wood and water. The Anglo expeditionists sought something more than just bare sustenance as they crossed the Panhandle. They wrote that they missed the forests of their youth; rich as the prairie grasses were, with an abundance of game including buffalo, turkey, deer, antelope, black bear, and "partridges" (quail or prairie chickens), the llano had no shade. They complained that stalking the animals was difficult with no trees for hiding. The descriptions always carried the shadow of the reporter's past.

True also for the Spanish *entradas*, exploratory journeys, of Francisco Vazquez de Coronado (1541–44), Juan Oñate (1601), Pedro Vial (1786 and 1788), and the Facundo Melgares party of 1806, except that these men harkened from a Spain of pampas. Theirs was a visceral comfort and their accounts registered an adventurer's as well as a metaphorist's curiosity. Despite hardships that befell both the early Spanish and the later Anglo crossers, the land resonated differently in their bones. Yet they both saw the llano as inconsequential in human terms, a forgettable desert.

"Bones incandescent" is a description used by Nancy Newhall to capture the effect of the New Mexico desert. The wife of the photo historian and critic Beaumont Newhall, Nancy, an inveterate hiker, observed: "Noon in the desert is a vast blaze overhead and a hard glow below. You're shut in by vast distances of light. You walk in the focus of the sun's rays. You are clothed in sun; sun glows in your blood, until even your bones feel incandescent."

What is the distance between sustenance and settlement, and how is it traveled, I wonder this bone-deep 100-degree August day as I stand at the first big mudded loop of the Middle Alamosa Creek, north about five miles from Tom's camp. There are trees in the Canadian Breaks—lots of them due east in what is called the Cedar Breaks, a badlands dotted with juniper (not cedar). That was another difference between the Spanish conquistadores and the American expeditions: the former followed the river and its tributaries and springs; the latter more the contour of the land, seeking manageable routes for future trade, wagon roads, railroads. The flatlands. No water. No wood.

Middle Alamosa Creek and Valley, Cedar Breaks. *Author photo.*

Here the Middle Alamosa widens and deepens, shimmying out
a thoroughfare of flat, pebbled sand and dun-mudded shale banks.
The now solidified beds look as if some giant animal squirmed on
his back, hollowing out the loops of the watercourse. Myth lives
here. The creek's strength and age, the persistence of water in a near
desert landscape, shows in the twenty-foot cut and the sprawling
width, maybe forty feet. Major Stephen Harriman Long, born in New
Hampshire, in 1820 the first American explorer to enter the Panhandle, led what originated as the Yellowstone Expedition, a military,
commercial, diplomatic, and scientific project. Due to cost cutting,
Congress in 1820 redirected the expedition's path to cross prairies and
survey the headwaters of the Platte, the Arkansas, and the Red Rivers.
Descending the Rocky Mountains, Long encountered the Canadian
River, mistaking it for the Red, correcting his error only when he
reached the confluence of the Canadian and the Arkansas. Dr. Edwin
James, one of the noted scientists on the expedition, commented
that "the river bed in front of our camp was . . . sixty yards in width,
twenty of which were naked sandbar, the remaining forty covered
with water, having the average depth of about ten inches. The current

is moderate, the water intensely red." In another account he described Ute Creek (a tributary of the Canadian) as containing brackish water, suspended with a quantity of red earth "so as to give it the colour of florid blood." No wonder the confusion was thorough: the Kiowa the Long party met along the way corroborated the mistaken Red River. Yes, of course, they nodded to Long: *Guadal P'a* is the Kiowa word for the Canadian River, which translates as Red River.

If the sun radiates in your bones, the ever-reddening mudflats seep vascularly. I love these changes in color as I walk along. Back on the farm, along the draws, the thickness of buffalo grass and side oats grama carpets the land until it pitches deeper and deeper into its eroding revelations. Grasses give way with the topsoil; darker, richer loams to colorful clays. The canyons I first discovered earlier in the summer, with their sandstone and shale sides of ochre, purple, and orange (faded of course, not bright, but subtle) impress, but the creek bed transforms.

I once ran atop time. It was all space for me along the roadways of the draws. On a particular June morning after a clarifying rain, I dodged puddles of water on my run. Sky above, but more sky below in the reflections of lingering clouds and blue on blue in the puddles, I had the dizzying feeling of tripping across the sky. Looking down into the water I could see sky; I ran on this mirror, yet my pace was of the steadying dirt-packed earth.

Is the distance between sustenance and settlement that of the relationship between space and place? Or is place merely the personal shape of time?

I have come some distance myself on the Middle Alamosa. I did not give birth or bury a child, as one woman did on the Whipple expedition, nor was I attacked by the Pawnee like Long, nor shad-owed by the Kiowa and Comanche, whose antipathy for Texans would have disastrously identified me sooner or later. I may share more with the pre-Columbian people whose ruins and hunting camps dot the Middle Alamosa Creek and many of the tributaries and the Canadian itself. They were hunters, but also farmers. They are the disappeared. No human account of them exists. Their arti-facts, their settlements, are fleeting in that they left no considerable civilization like the Anasazi or Mimbres. Their story is folded within

Jogging road, Armitage Farms, top of North Draw. *Author photo.*

the landscape. They were present for perhaps three hundred years along the Canadian Breaks. Theirs was a life both of bare survival and of brief settlement, but mostly the conduits of the Canadian were a temporary stop along a road of necessary movement and change.

A refuge.

⋎ I decide to re-enter the creek bed, walking along bottom now, nothing visible but sky and towering banks. What would have happened had the explorers tried thinking like a river? Donald Worcester writes in his *River of Empire: Water, Aridity, and the Growth of the American West* that rivers, creeks, watersheds exercise rationale as part of nature forever on the move. Worcester characterizes the nature of water as "mobile, elusive, relentless, and vulnerable" in its "fundamental rationality" of finding the easiest way ultimately to the sea. This will of water surrounds me, a cranium of cobbled decisions. I wonder at the decision of a looping bend, a meandering Worcester says make sense. No wasted motion here. To learn from this time-worn source would be to live by the water cycle. At Paint Rock, at Rocky Dell, so evidenced as true. As a basic pattern of life and death, a return to the source of being, the water cycle—like the Awanyu of Paint Rock—is ancient metaphor. As Worchester observes, what scientists added to this sacred pattern is the notion that the movement of water is unending—an undiminished loop that when studied can serve as a model for understanding the entire economy of nature.

What I see is a dry creek bed, deeply worn. The Middle Alamosa ran out of its water several miles back when the last trickle disappeared into the sand. But the memory of water registers all along these banks and bottom: dry mud slides striking a vulnerable angle of repose, the fickle equilibrium of small Ogallala stones poised on the fragile ledges; the creek bed rub-board smooth, coursing of previous runoffs wrinkled into the sandstone plane. Here a scraggly juniper root juts an arthritic finger from the eroded surface; there a wayward cactus teeters on a blanched edge. Soil wants to stay and water wants to go. The result is a story of conveyances. I listen with eyes opening to this narrative of communication and transport.

We do not speak this language well, we humans. "Upright among staring fish," as Robert Lowell described us, we moderns have built "hydraulic societies"—based on hierarchical power garnered from capturing, diverting, controlling water. The more industrialized we become, the more we contest the will of water, opposing, obstructing with often dire outcome, such as the Aswan Dam, which has collected and blocked the silts historically fertilizing the Nile Valley. Dams in general have led to artificial fertilizers and pesticides, irrigation, and practices designed for immediate results, not long-range sensitivity to the limits of the water cycle. Perhaps the most disastrous result of our ignoring the water cycle is an alienation from the land and its stream of life—leading, of course, to more objectifying control.

Author in deep cut of Middle Alamosa Creek. *Courtesy Randy Roark.*

Nora Tilden writes in *Biography* that "places . . . pretend to be blank, though beneath any place is everything that has ever happened there." Looking at the cliff's temporal striations, I want to feel profoundly parented, standing here upright within the ceaseless horizontals of river-think, a vertical creature in need of adoption: mother earth, father sky.

One of the nineteenth-century explorers, James Abert, had an artist's eye that allowed him some intimacy with the Canadian Breaks. Producing accurate maps and illustrated journals, he entered the west Panhandle north of the Canadian in 1845, with orders from the U.S. government to make a reconnaissance along the Canadian River through the country of the Kiowa and Comanche. Following the river's course—along the south bank in Oldham County until he dropped down to hit the north fork of the Red River—he surveyed tributaries and springs, documenting animal, plant, and bird life.

He established cordial relations with both Comanche and Kiowa, heeding Indian traces, which followed the watercourses, as he made his way.

Beyond the government directives, those explorers who employed Indian guides and Indian knowledge acted on the "reason" of water cycles. In 1840, Josiah Gregg blazed a southern route along the Canadian, which became known as the Fort Smith (Arkansas) to Santa Fe Trail, by intersecting well-used tributary streams where wood and water could be had. He wrote *Commerce of the Prairies* popularizing this southern route; in the summer of 1849 as many as two thousand travelers followed it. Tracking this route in April of 1849, Capt. Randolph B. Marcy acted as escort for eighteen wagons, one six-pounder iron gun, and a traveling forge drawn by six mules. He employed a physician, twenty-six dragoons, and fifty men of the Fifth Infantry for safe passage of his "emigrants." The Gold Rush had begun in California, requiring guarded travel through Comanche and Kiowa territory.

I know his trail, still visible on my neighbor Kim Montgomery's land. When the daylight is right you can see the faint impression of narrow wagon wheels, especially if you climb in the back of a pickup to gain some height. Both Gregg and Marcy crossed about three miles northwest of Vega, recording sweet spring water and copious grapes and plums at what had to be Kim's springs—the "no name springs" where Randy and I walked—feeding the Middle Alamosa. Tilden reminds us: "Places . . . pretend to be blank. . . . To write such a place is not . . . simply to inscribe the place onto a page. . . . [T]o write a place is to lay across it a skin, a membrane of text and experience. The skin is there to hold the stories of the place in place, transforming the illegible (because shapeless) land into a storied landscape. Land becomes landscape once humans have touched it—once it contains and embodies our stories."

Marcy's landscape followed Gregg's and even Abert's—men for whom nature's economy was written as the promise of settlement, development, a railroad line to the Pacific, a short cut to the Gold Coast. Their stories are those of passage, not refuge. An undeniable trope of each of these stories is the life-defying and -threatening, the fearsome Llano Estacado. Whether an unchartable "sea of grass" or a desert wasteland, the llano was uninhabitable, necessarily to be carefully skirted, passed by. Despite the regimens of West Point—educated topographers, geologists, military men, engineers—none could imagine the llano as an extension of the habitat of water and wood. None could see it as one of the largest plateaus in America, carved by the erosion of water cycles, one of which is now called Canadian. Or that it was home for those who lived within its cycles, not merely passing over it. Nor could they imagine what lay beneath their membrane of stories—the source, one of the largest underground "rivers" in the world, the Ogallala Aquifer.

I follow the dry streambed, amazed at its depth and width. Like the wagon trains of old, I climb out every once in a while to the flatlands, to get my bearings, to see my place in its story.

⋎ I look at Mother's brain—the x-ray of it—and see no indication of the condition the doctor before me describes. "Clearly, she has a hydrocephalic condition," Dr. Mitchell drones on. "You know, what people used to call 'water on the brain.'"

"But I thought that was a child's disease—or, er—condition? Is that what you would call it—a condition?"

"Yes, children can develop it, but it occurs quite frequently in the elderly."

My mother is sitting calmly, almost blankly, in a nearby chair. She brightens and smiles her cooperative smile whenever the doctor turns toward her.

I'm not comfortable with this talking about my mother in front of her, as if she is not there, or is too out of it to hear or understand.

"So, what does this mean?" I continue to Dr. Mitchell, someone I like who seems tender with Mother but has all doctors' practical tone.

"Well, her weaving on her walker, for instance. That's a sign of the imbalance of signals in the brain. Hydrocephalic conditions put pressure on certain parts of the brain as fluids collect there. These pressures interfere with normal brain function and can affect ambulation, decision making, memory, even speech."

Mother had been weaving for months now, veering a hard left, as if driving on a low tire. She had fallen repeatedly, and this led to my having to move her from her hometown of sixty-eight years, first to an independent living facility but now to assisted living. Mother had lived alone for fifteen years, and despite an alarm she wore (mostly) around her neck, when she fell, she forgot to push the button.

Mother being Mother, we laughed when she bore left as I gently guided her back on track. We were an inebriated-looking tandem, going down the hall. The falls were not laughable; they were scary. But we *did* laugh about the falls. This is what Mother and I did. We made light of her aging, of the unspoken grief, which she never publicly expressed, over my dad's death.

"Mother, are you on another diet?" I would ask, knowing she loved to eat (a kind of compensation), but tried to diet too.

"Lucky you have that padding around you so when you fall you can just bounce to the phone and call me."

"Mother, you *are* gaining weight. You look like you swallowed a flying saucer."

"Mother, have you been hitting that wine again?" (Joking about the wayward walker. My mother was a teetotaler.)

Mother would giggle like a little girl. She never lost that little girl affect that always drew people to her. Now a shade under five feet, and still pretty, a diamond-shaped face, olive skin, curly grey (but dyed auburn) hair, and carefully kept nails and dress, Mother was a charmer. Always had been. Always would be.

She continued to charm me—and the doctors.

"Dorothy," Dr. Mitchell said, finally turning to Mother. "There's a surgery we can do for this. We put a shunt in your brain to drain the excess water out. It's what's commonly done," she added looking at me.

Mother nods, always complicit when it comes to doctors, though this one, a female, she had resisted on occasion. The surgeon, Dr. Mitchell continued to explain, would be a specialist—a man, so I knew my mother would agree.

Later though, talking only to me, Dr. Mitchell was surprisingly forthright in her opinion. "The success rate is about fifty/fifty in these cases, with someone your mother's age and in her condition. The shunts can become infected, requiring future surgery. And of course this is brain surgery, not without risks. Anesthesia always has a negative effect, sometimes lasting. You may want to talk with others who have had this procedure or their caregivers. If she were my mother . . ."

Reading between the lines, I was surprised that Dr. Mitchell did not recommend this surgery.

I consulted with another doctor, a neurologist and surgeon who agreed to discuss the procedure with me. He was cavalier about the operation and whipped a long tubing out of his desk to demonstrate the plumbing that would be put in Mother's brain and drain out through her bladder.

"So what are the consequences if we don't have this surgery?" I haltingly asked, nervous about either side of the fifty/fifty.

"She'll just get worse. The water will continue to build pressure and that will eventually affect everything—mobility, speech, eating. If she gets a severe headache, we need to know immediately. It may take a while. She'll die."

I already knew: either choice, water would have its way.

⋁ So I hiked. I hiked and hiked. The Middle Alamosa was a weekend destination, with trips maybe two or three times during the week in the summer. I hiked and I mulled. Mostly I tried to escape. Making life-determining decisions for my mother was a constant source of stress. What could I learn here that would steady me? I picked up a red-striated Alibates scraper, with a smooth thumb hold; it doubled as a worry stone. I felt displaced.

Part of it was the loss of my childhood home, along with my mother too. When I had to move Mother, I also needed to sell the house I grew up in in order to have enough money to care for her. Retirement homes were expensive. My parents' combined Social Security payment was small; the tiny farm income provided the rest. No matter how cute and girlish Mother seemed, she was a strong and willful woman. She resisted my advice. Her mother, my grandmother "Mama Dunn," had raised her six children—three girls, three boys—as a single mother. Her husband—my never-to-be-known grandfather, James Dunn—had abandoned the family when they moved from east Texas to Amarillo during the Depression. Mama Dunn worked in a cleaners to support the family. All the children tried to leave and support themselves as soon as they could, the boys striking out on their own, the girls marrying young. After years of bending over a steam press, Mama Dunn actually bought a modest house of her own. I remember visiting her at work, calling back to her through the heavy heated air of the cleaners.

I recall secret hiding places in her house, like the hall closet. While the arborvitae grew until they blocked the sidewalk to the front door (something, Washington Irving–like, I didn't realize until one day after her death when the house sold and I noticed the trees had been cut back), I read piles of comic books under the single light bulb of the closet. I read everything, Blondie and Dagwood, Superman, the Green Hornet. The domestic comedies bored me; I preferred the adventure strips. My grandmother was still poor, but she had "magazines" and a stubbornness that she passed on to her daughter.

I also hid away in her gardening shed out back in the yard. Her old bonnets and spades comforted me, the earth smell something I connected with my green-thumb grandmother. I wanted to inhabit that smell. There was something mysterious about her. The family story was that she could remove warts, that she held a secret come down through her Irish/Cherokee forebears, a secret passed on only through the women of the family. I believed. When I was a girl, she touched the wart on my finger and it went away. I wanted the secret to come to me through my mother, the power of some native roots.

But mother worked her magic on dresses, drapes, quilts, breakfast, lunch, and dinner. When my dad died in 1989, she immediately manned the desk, finding a local young farmer to lease the farm, tending to business. She had worked at the bank, after all, taking that job so that she could be home from work about the time I came home from school. She was smart, a quick study, adapting easily to a computer world, popular in Vega where the kids called her "Lady Bank." Like my dad, she should have gone to college, but neither family had the resources. Both channeled their intelligence and gifts into civic and church activities. She dispersed candy and suckers at the drive-in window when the clients drove through.

But her stoicism hid the grief of losing my dad and never really abated—she was obviously depressed—and despite my push for her to talk to someone, perhaps take a course on grief management, she pretended she was okay, soldiering on. She was a willing victim of several telemarketing scams, at one point writing a ten thousand dollar check to something called "Drug-Free America." For this she received what

I assured her was a fake certificate. I began listening on the other line in her house when someone suspicious would call. (I hated doing this!) I got their information and then called the Better Business Bureau in whatever state the scam artist was calling from. In every case, Mother poured money down a black hole. Both my parents had been frugal and sensible about money—despite the Depression, never in debt. This maddened me—my mother's willful destruction of herself through inane expenditures, making it even harder to care for her. And my blood pressure, for the first time in my life, went up. There was simply not enough money for her to throw any away.

Men happened by, offering to resurface her driveway, which did not need it. She overpaid. Someone trimmed her trees—badly and for an extravagant fee. The years wore on. I worried. She seemed not to.

Then the Vega bank "failed." This business had been the pride and joy of my family. It had enjoyed the highest banking ratings, survived the Depression without closing. My dad, civic-minded and a leader in the small town, served as vice president and had been a past president of the Texas Bankers Association, repeatedly offered jobs at large banks downstate. He was a natural leader. People trusted and relied on him. At his funeral, several businessmen stood to give testimony that his faith in them had enabled their success. While my dad was still in the bank, before he retired after fifty years, the then president brought his son-in-law into the bank with the intention of naming him president. Both Dad and the other vice president, Jim Haliburton, a family friend, advised against this. Roy, the son-in-law, was a game warden who had no knowledge of banking or finances. Years later, after my dad had retired and passed away, the bank failed when it was discovered that several million dollars had been laundered through a feed lot scam. The directors—mostly older men well established in Oldham County—were clueless; Roy, the son-in-law made bank president, had kept two sets of books. No matter how obvious this embezzlement, and the fact that the missing millions did not "break" the bank, Roy escaped with a light, country-club prison sentence while the directors were held responsible for the missing money. The bank never closed, but the FDIC would not honor the stockholders' investment, selling the bank to another entity, declaring the former stock void.

Overnight my mother lost the one investment my dad was able to muster through years of a low-paying job at a rural bank. She also lost face. The gregarious and beloved Dorothy stayed home, ordered more and more on the phone, dropped out. None of the bank situation was her fault, nor was it connected to her in any way—and no one blamed her—but the shock was like a death. And like my dad's, she hid it too. The last straw was when the Sunday school class she taught decided to disband, mostly because she continually showed up late.

Dorothy. Dorothy Mae. Mama. What are you doing?

This particular day, distraught at the balancing act that went on in my mind ceaselessly, I grab water and the truck keys and head north. I decide to drive through Green's ranch to a deep canyon on Mansfield's where the Middle Alamosa makes its most daring meander. Am I beginning to do crazy things like my mother? No jack, no spare. The pickup with 145,000 miles on its rickety chassis. I don't care. I hid my grief over my dad's death too, running off to Paris to meet my then man friend right after the funeral. Rushing back, breathless but unflappable in my university classroom. I didn't let the shirttail hit my back, as they say down at the post office, even as my heart was breaking.

The road narrows as I cross the Middle Alamosa on a dry wash and angle uphill, parking near an escarpment. Once out of the sketchy grass cover, I spot a piece of worked flint, then next to it on a gravelly ledge, a piece of corded pottery.

People seem to think the "history" of the area begins with the cowboy days or the ranching era, but the Canadian River Valley is rich in pre-Columbian sites. What once were called Plains Pueblo people and now the Antelope Creek Phase people populated the Canadian area from the eastern Panhandle west into New Mexico, the farthest west known site being close to San Jon, New Mexico, about fifty miles west of Vega. This was a transitional group, moving from a hunter-gatherer culture to mixed agriculture. Considerable archaeological evidence has appeared since the first excavations of the 1920s, but the Antelope Creek people are commonly unknown except to experts and enthusiasts. The corded ware—modest, thick, brown, undecorated pottery, except for the imprinted lines—appears to be strictly utilitarian. Perhaps there was no time or inspiration for decoration in a life so harsh. Prior to the Antelope Creek Phase folks, Clovis and Folsom points signal one of the oldest cultures in North America, dating some nine thousand years ago. A major Folsom site was discovered in 1908 west of Dalhart by one of the early black cowboys, George McJunken, and Clovis sites in the early twentieth century near Clovis, New Mexico, at Blackwater Draw. With atlatls and spears, these people felled the enormous *Bison antiquus*, much larger than the contemporary buffalo, and the prehistoric mastodons. The killing fields were often water holes, particularly playas, where the animals could be cornered by a group of hunters. Points and spears from both these cultures have been found along the Middle Alamosa Creek, which lies approximately halfway between these major sites. Thus the general area is central to some of the earliest cultures of North America. The later Antelope Creek Phase proto-archaic people made hunting camps on the canyon edge—an extension of more developed villages and a vantage point for spotting buffalo.

I pocket the pottery shard for good luck. Someone made a life here. Someone shaped this stone-like clay. Though there is still no fingerprint, the clay had been kneaded, pinched, marked with a fiber. I savor this connection.

It's quiet, getting late. I made a late start. It's not quite the crepuscular time of skunk, badger, bobcat, and cougar, but the wind has died down and the light lingers yellow in the west. It's as if the land holds its breath before exhaling into the night. I linger when I should drive. The silence is such that a buzz sets in my ears—a ringing from within held by the lassitude without. Time doesn't stand still. But I do, for the first time in weeks, permeated with nature, the calm settling in for the night.

This must be what Keith Basso refers to in *Wisdom Sits in Places: Landscape and Language among the Western Apache*, where he recounts the advice given him by White Mountain Apache elders. It has to do with our restless minds. Basso's informant tells him "wisdom sits in places" and if one heeds this wisdom, he will have "a smooth mind" like water, that is, calm, without worry. The wisdom of place, like the thinking river, is about emplacement, something the Navajo describe as being "in place." It's not simple physical being but a being conscious of the storied place, of all that has gone before it, of the natural layers and the membranes laid down through time.

Years before, back when Hands Across America occurred, I decided to go to the pueblo just north of Albuquerque where there is an interpretative center and an old kiva you're allowed to enter. I wanted to see what that occasion would feel like there. There was no one there but an elderly Pueblo man at the desk. I descended into the kiva—still, musty, faint paintings on the wall. These were of the style of the Bison Run shaman, I now realize, of the Awanyu at Paint Rock. Handprints dotted the walls. My breath slowed; I couldn't feel my heart beat. I was near the center of something I could never name, something not my own. And of course, I was not alone.

But the sneaky ego interrupts and here on the edge of the Middle Alamosa's deepest canyon, a smugness sweeps over me. No, I am alone, and this is my experience. How fortunate, but still it is mine. Just as my ego expands with this exceptionalness, this sole witnessing, I hear a low whir. At first I ignore it. But the sound intensifies, moves, so that I realize something is out there besides the *chip chip* of the mockingbird in the mesquite nearby. I rarely have encountered anyone on my hikes through Green's and into Mansfield's—not even a ranch manager. But someone is out there on the road. I don't want my privacy violated, I don't want to feel exposed—the spell of calmness and belonging broken. So I weave down below the extended ledge so I can squat and watch. I begin to see myself as a poor stand-in in a B-western—a female, unarmed, and in tennis shoes. Several minutes pass and something emerges on the road.

It's a seismographic team, each in a Rhino, those persistent ATVs that can take you anywhere. All of a sudden I think of them not as "seizmos" but as "gizmos"—a string of them, a comical convoy. From my hiding place, they look like toys, holdovers from *Star Wars*, moving over the desert landscape. I'm instantly annoyed too. This was my reverie, my special place. Mine, mine!!!!

I know that oil rig operations have been going on since the 1950s here on Mansfield's. Some people used to say the Greens ran cattle and old man Mansfield ran oil rigs. There was some truth (and envy perhaps) in this gossip.

But surely I am having the last laugh—here in the bush, hidden away, watching them. They are encased in their technology; they don't "get it." They are emissaries of unrelenting development. I note there are more new roads than ever trailing to new oil fields. Son Bobby Mansfield, who hadn't lived on the ranch since a boy, enjoyed the ever-developing fruits of his dad's early vision. Meanwhile, between oil development, that use of water, and the sand and gravel pits that dot the ranches, the natural tributary drainage is constantly compromised, not to mention the unmeasurable beauty of the place. Why cherish or restore a landscape whose stories are unknown? I think about the single, forlorn juniper, which has managed to seed itself atop one of the largest gravel pit areas nearby. Landmark—of what? What the maps identify rightfully as "strip mining."

They pass. Peace returns. I make a swing down on the canyon edge to look over. Something orange and trailing, something irregular in the landscape catches my eye. The "seizmos" aren't gone after all. Trailing down into the canyon from a large plug standing upright above is an orange electric cord. The place is plugged in. If it were earlier in the day, I would have followed the extension cord down into the canyon. I have a notion of pulling the plug like some character in an Edward Abbey novel. I had my warning earlier but refused to acknowledge it. Miles of thick black hose run through the ranch, conveying water to the oil wells. Large man-made tanks, often covered in black plastic tarps, stand as reservoir way stations along these lines. Development. Using water in a water-starved landscape, endangering bird life. Use, not kinship.

Time to go. My water is out too. I head back to the truck. And this is where I have my reckoning. The left front tire is nearly flat. Singularly blessed with the wilderness experience? No spare. No jack. Flashing before my mind: how many miles to town? Can I really sleep in the small cab? No water. Now where are those damn "seizmos" when you need them? In a flash, I am in the truck, wrestling the front end already pulling to the left. Maybe I can catch them.

First hill. No men. Second wash. No little green men. With dark now coming on, I whip the resisting truck over each hill, bank each curve like a crazy racecar driver. Gun the motor, gear down, spin out through sand. I know I am on the losing end of a Roadrunner cartoon. Coyote. At one point I even strip the nob off the aging gearshift, sticking it back hastily where first was reverse. If I could just make it to Highway 385, I could flag down help. I haven't hit the rim yet.

I make it to Vega. About a mile from my house the Jeep dips dangerously to the left and I grind to a stop off the roadway. The tire is completely flat. I'd hit the rim. I gather my stuff and walk the uneventful dark distance home but emptied of the addled mind that started the day.

⚡ I continue to look for evidence of the Antelope Creek Phase people. The ledge on Mansfield's likely was a "sub homestead," one of three kinds of settlements along the Middle Alamosa and the Canadian. According to the one archaeological reconnaissance study focused on the Middle Alamosa, the three classes of architectural sites were multiple family hamlets of twenty or more "residential rooms," single family homesteads, and sub homesteads in the field—hut sites that lacked residential rooms. From their central residential locations, these people extended hunting and trading through the other kinds of sites. As many as forty varied sites were recorded along the Middle Alamosa alone.

They sought out high places for refuge and protection. The cliffs and ledges all along the Middle Alamosa embedded their secrets. Surface lithics recorded by William Marmaduke and Hayden Whitsett in their survey of the Middle Alamosa in 1964 were merely the random letters of a story still untold. Where had they migrated from exactly? Where had they gone, and why? The lithics and pottery situated them from around 1200 to the late 1400s A.D. along these mesas and valleys. The older settlements tended to be contiguous room rather than single-room dwellings. That fact and the wealth of trade items suggest the more recent and smaller settlements engaged in considerable trade. By 1350 A.D. the more recent sites yielded an increase of 4,600 percent in trade items such as painted Southwest pueblo pottery, turquoise beads and pendants, obsidian nodules and tools, marine-shell beads, and other objects. Collared-rim ceramic vessels and Niobrara jasper suggest trade from the Central Plains; rare Caddoan ceramics show east Texas influences. At some burial sites, unbroken Mogollon pots have been recovered, suggesting contact with the Jornado Mogollon of southern New Mexico.

Here was a nexus of activity, a hub drawing exchange from north, south, east, and west, its spokes reaching outward. What the Antelope Creek Phase people traded was buffalo—meat, skin, bones,

Landergin Mesa, Mansfield's Ranch. *Author photo.*

tools—and the places they found the buffalo were atop high cliffs and mesas, along tributaries, near springs.

One of the most spectacular and humbling of these sites is Landergin Mesa, or Arrowhead Mesa, as it is called locally. It is east of the Middle Alamosa but within its 21,000-acre drainage, near the confluence of Ranch Creek and Billy's Creek, which on some maps become the East Alamosa Creek. Nearby rippled layers of hard sandstone suggest earlier springs activity along these watercourses. Landergin Mesa rises some 140 feet from the flat plain that surrounds it, like a stark and lone pyramid. A sloping inverted V form, capped with an erosion-resistant sandstone from the Trujillo Formation of the Upper Triassic period, it seems to shift in the ranges of light from daylight to dark. From the approaching road, it disappears at times due to changes in elevation; from the low places mesquite and cactus obscure its view.

I climb. My knees are worn from my thirty years of jogging, but I want to see the Middle Alamosa Valley from the Antelope Creek perspective. The climb is difficult: loose rocks, sliding shale challenging my footholds. I have a bit of agoraphobia too; I look up, not down, and zigzag my way up. Breaching the cap is not easy. Refuge, yes, and defense.

On top, the view is a stunning 360 degrees of the Middle Alamosa watershed. If Landergin hides from our view on the ground, here it provides a thirteenth-century Native's version of a topographic map. I see where I have come from, the slithering cuts through time. To the north is my future, the remaining two and a half miles to the bluish purple river horizon. It's windy and hot and hard up here. Winters must have struck bone deep. The architecture—now faint from vandalism, excavation, and infill—consists of stone rooms, horizontal stones laid on vertical formations, most rectangular and approximately 135–650 square feet at the largest, some partial rooms on the edges of the mesa indicating erosion on the sides. Typical Antelope Creek residential rooms were built a foot or so below ground level, with interior roof support around a central hearth. Elevated activity areas or benches flanked the depressed "channel" that ran east-west through the central third of the room. Rooms could contain a dais or platform altar, located within the channel or in the west wall. Entryways were low for crawling or stooping to enter. Little of this is obvious with infill and grass reclaiming the mesa top.

A virtual Who's Who of archaeologists, beginning with Warren King Moorehead and Floyd Studer in 1920 or 1921, visited the freestanding mesa. Moorehead reported twenty-two small circular structures. Studer returned several times, in 1929 with Dr. Ronald J. Olsen of the American Museum of Natural History. Olsen also noted isolated circular structures measuring six feet in diameter. Ted Sayles came in 1932, collecting a number of surface artifacts, including trade items. In 1951 Jack Hughes made five visits, which resulted in details of over one hundred rooms measuring fifteen to twenty feet in diameter. By 1959, he noted considerable vandalism, which he connected with the intense oil exploration activities on the ranch. The National Park Service listed the site as a National Historic Landmark in 1964, adding it to the National Register of Historic Places in 1966: "one of the largest, best stratified, least damaged, and most spectacularly located ruins of panhandle culture." That plaque is overgrown by mesquite and dense brush at the bottom of the mesa. But atop Landergin, along with whatever sleeps here, is another plaque "honoring" one of the local pot-hunters, hoisted onto the mesa by prankster friends. There was an attempt to make Landergin, and nearby Saddleback Mountain, a state park, but individual landowner resistance and the logistics of getting to the site from a major highway assured that the proposal languished.

When archaeologist Chris Lintz, working for the Texas Historical Commission, excavated a forty-two-square meter area near the east edge in 1983–84, he found ten isolated one-room structures from seven stratified components. Carbon dating confirmed the educated guesses of previous surveying archaeologists: Landergin Mesa had been continuously occupied for at least three hundred years. But one outstanding fact distinguishes it from the many excavated sites ranging from New Mexico, across the Texas Panhandle, and into Oklahoma: most of the houses were built as isolated structures, rather than the typical contiguous rooms expected with such limited space atop the mesa. Landergin Mesa served as a refuge rather than a permanent village.

↓ I return to Landergin again and again. It helps me appreciate erosion. Standing on its sandstone top, I feel strangely sheltered, despite the wind that could sweep me away. I stand on fine conglomerate riverbed sediments, higher now than the surrounding eroded valley that water etched away. Across the east chasm I see a canyon cliff where I once sat mesmerized by the shifting mesa at dusk. It shares Landergin's age—the Upper Triassic period—compared to the older valley. What was once low becomes high—like memory, a surfacing of time passed, yet present. I continue to search for a sign of the women's lives—a pottery shard with a fingerprint. I find scrapers instead, "guitar-pick" scrapers, edges chipped sharp for skinning, cutting meat, with a thumb hold— slight impression—smooth as skin.

Back home, Mother's mind succumbs to its own river. Her hydrocephalic condition worsens; at first she can't walk, and now she can't talk. When the attendants at the assisted living recommended she move to the Alzheimer's wing (when she still walked, she exited the building a few times "to go shopping," which they construed as sign of the disease), I dug out the x-ray that confirmed dementia and moved her to a group home, where she could get good individual care.

I hire a woman to come play a portable piano and sing with the residents. My mother can't talk, she can't sing, but she appreciates the music and understands when you talk to her. Halfway through the hymn everyone, including the accompanist, stops. They can't remember the next stanza. And somehow into that silence comes a tiny, isolated, quaking soprano voice singing not only the missing line, but the rest of the hymn.

CHAPTER FOUR

Circling

Season of the sunflowers—that's the time in late August just before the monarch butterflies arrive, the bittersweet few days before I leave the farm for the university four hundred miles away. Along the county road that borders the farm and cuts across the draw common to Kim's ranch and Armitage Farms, those tall, spindly wild sunflowers hum with insects as they wave in the ever-present wind. Their relatives—the giant sunflowers grown for oil—mind their diurnal ways. I see them at the nearby agricultural farm following the sun, craning necks between day and night. But these renegades, the wild ones, just turn willy-nilly, free until some dutiful county employee mows them down. A month or so later would assure seeds and cover for wildlife. The bar ditches are rich in wildflowers even in drought time, if you wait long enough. Ditches are water catchers and conveyers; they drain into the draw. I'm sustained by the wildflowers' stubborn persistence.

Mother's birthday is August 22, and I am always conflicted by the need to leave before her big day to return to my job. Summer isn't over according to the sunflowers, and the school calendars don't fit what you feel in your bones, either. What makes sense to me on the prairie—the cycles of animals, plants, temperature, rain, slight changes in storm patterns, the color of the sky at midday—becomes an illogical journey southwest to desert El Paso, a different summer.

So on August 20 we have a little early celebration for her. Doris, the live-in caregiver at the group home, insists on preparing Mother's favorite: Mexican food. A southerner who knows her gravies and how to stretch a meal, Doris puts together some unidentifiable casserole that passes for the enchiladas Mother savors. Doris is a dear, always caring and helpful, genuine in her love of the residents. But Doris can be trying too. She likes to talk, needs to because she has only the elderly ladies for companions, so when I arrive she launches into some tall tale—maybe to impress, maybe because she is lonely. Maybe because Doris lives in another world.

Today the story has to do with Eddie Murphy. To hear Doris tell it, she'd dated Eddie Murphy when she lived in California. But then again she had written lyrics for Willie Nelson songs. She often got on very negative tracks, recounting scoundrel husbands, disappearing children, discrimination at jobs. She told these stories without so much as a breath taken; I could only nod, accomplice to a fabrication that made me uneasy. I was living on another planet too. The planet of lies and abductions.

I had settled into my caregiving mode, embraced it, put Mother as my number one priority, choosing a place I could confidently leave her. I simply couldn't relocate her to El Paso (so many new doctors to find, none of her friends there, I'd need a sitter with her when I was at work), and I had my profession to keep up with. But I didn't settle without a fight. When my dad died, I remember feeling a terror: my mother would now depend on me as if I were his replacement. There were unspoken expectations of what a daughter should do. I was independent, and maybe because I wasn't married (though there were serious relationships), I had lived mostly on my own since college days. My life was private, separate from my parents, even though we always were extremely close. I valued my chosen freedom, yet now felt sadness, aching love, and deep responsibility for my mother. The fight was within myself—wanting to run, take a job overseas, disappear into a far-flung state. Mostly I feared my inability to make the life-and-death health decisions for Mother; I'd had little experience with the medical world and felt ill-equipped to knowledgably and emotionally shepherd Mother through the ever-pressing protocols of the health care business. I lost the fight—or won it. I quit my tenure-track full professorship in Hawai'i and came back to Texas, to a university as close as I could get in order to "help take care" of Mother. Eight hundred miles, round-trip. A difficult weekend jaunt. But not as far as Honolulu.

Roy, my older brother by nine years, lived relatively near Vega with his family off and on throughout the years. Once, when he was changing jobs, my parents raised his oldest son for a year, putting him in the first grade at Vega. But now Roy was in Katy, Texas, on the outskirts of Houston, eight driving hours away. He seemed always to be working—as did the entire family: my sister-in-law and the two sons. Of course they were! They were busy. I was the daughter, single, a college professor (surely a cushy job, right?). It was predictable. The care of Mother—her health, her finances, her emotional state—and the farm, fell completely to me.

Mother is "pouching" her food; she's holding it in her cheeks, without swallowing. This is something new, something that follows the knee replacements, the foot surgeries, the breast cancer, the bladder cancer, the loss of ambulation and speech. Doris and I have been feeding her for a while now; her tremors are so bad the food flies off her fork. She's tied into her chair; she's gotten so thin. She slips incrementally down during meals, almost disappearing before the birthday cake. Now she seems unable to swallow. The meal appears a bust, but Mother smiles her sweet smile and Doris makes her an Ensure shake.

When she's back in her recliner, I eye Mother's hair. It has been dyed a carrot orange, her precious, natural curls shorn to almost a burr cut. It's difficult getting any hairdressers to come to the group home, where there might be only one client. The lady who comes engages in crazy Doris talk the entire time, dyeing and clipping as she goes. The last time I was there, I had to stop my urge to rush to the rescue as both jabbering women lowered Mother nonchalantly backward into the tub in order to wet her hair.

"Mother, you look like Queen Elizabeth." Of course I mean the carrot-top Elizabeth, the one with the smothering ruff. Her hair looks like the "beautician" took a lawn mower to it.

Mother smiles her sweet little smile.

"Look Mom," I say, opening up today's newspaper. Mother loves the news, politics, and such.

"Look, we might have a woman president. Wouldn't that be great?"

Mother points a bony finger, shaking, into the page, like jabbing someone in the ribs. She points instead to a sale on shoes.

Sales first, then news, then politics.

When it's time to go, it's always the same. Her tiny hand becomes a vice on my wrist, resisting my departure.

"Gotta go back to work, Mom," I say, peeling back each finger gently. I try to keep upbeat even though I want to cry each time. "I'll be back soon. Maybe in a week." I'm held hostage by my love for her, which aches from some deep maternal and filial source. And I'll lie if it takes that to make her happy.

᚛ Make her happy. This is my greatest worry as I carry photos of the Middle Alamosa sights and a tiny, alabaster-like Alibates point back with me to school. I so want her to be happy, and who can tell? I feel guilty for her loneness, her physical condition, even though I do all I can to assuage it. Randy Roark had recovered the point from on top of Little Arrowhead Mesa, the smaller Antelope Creek Phase settlement just northwest of Landergin on a branch of West Alamosa Creek. It's a beautiful and precious treasure from the vandalized slopes. I need to keep an image of the high places, the patterns of refuge. I pin the topo map, now documented with hikes, dates, sightings, to my study wall in my condo in El Paso. "Remember," I say.

At some point I can't identify, Mother allowed herself to be swept along the tide of her own aging. She never complained through the breast cancer surgeries, or the two bladder cancer surgeries, each with the probing, humiliating follow-up treatments where attendants wore masks and the room bore signs warning of poison. The CAT scans, the full-body x-rays, the exploratory uterine scrape, the dye run through, the core biopsy, the bleeding: she bore them all, crying out only occasionally. The inner sweetness of the willful Dorothy Mae won out as Mother and I shared fried chicken (one of her favorites) and late-night television, first at the independent living, then the assisted living, and now the group home setting (except that Doris made us turn the TV off early). But at her age, ninety, she never made real friends anywhere; she always seemed to be waiting for me to return. I was the anchor. Donna and James, who owned and managed the group home, came to my rescue by taking Mother to the routine doctor's appointments when I couldn't get there from El Paso and checking on us both when Mother was in the hospital. They and the residents—Doris included—became my family. I ate at the

Randy Roark at Little Arrowhead Peak. *Author photo.*

table, ladling my Doris gravy to the side. I chatted with the old ladies as if they were best friends. This was my life, not some Fulbright somewhere. I couldn't continue to resist.

I knew this the day the mouse skittered across the kitchen floor while I lounged with my feet propped up on my study desk in the hall of my El Paso condo. Had it been only the kitchen, and only one mouse, I might have been calmer. But soon I was aware that a mouse was there, and zip, something that suspiciously looked like a mouse also just ran into the bedroom. I let it go for a while until at night I worried I might run into a furry creature on the way to the bathroom. Plain and simple: my condo had been invaded by mice.

Simple. We set traps, Tomás (the gardener and fix-it man at the condo) and I. Little or nothing happened except that more mice seemed to arrive. Finally, Tomás got down on the floor to peer under the sink and discovered a hole in the wall. The mice were breeding and spreading from inside the wall of the condo. This was no Saturday afternoon Tom and Jerry cartoon. Yikes indeed.

In the middle of this minor hysteria, which I tried increasingly to see as a resolvable scene out of *Fantasia* (the one where the water bucket endlessly spills), I realized Mother wasn't receiving her Social Security payment. I let that ride for a month too, not understanding the mysteries of Social Security any better than the reproduction of mice. Turns out they aren't so different. Repeated calls to Social Security turned up nothing, except that I could not act on Mother's behalf, even with my medical power of attorney. I thought I had all the documents I needed to take care of my mother, but I kept getting an endless loop of "information" from Social Security. One day I finally got to the bottom of that as I went in person to the Social Security Office in downtown El Paso and an employee, an Iraqi War vet, took pity on the lady in front of him near tears. As the mice flourished back at the condo, the attendant informed me that my mother was dead.

Deceased according to the Social Security records. "It's in the computer, ma'am. That's what it says."

I drove to Amarillo over the weekend, a migraine headache and high blood pressure in tow. What was the reproduction cycle of "house" mice? I would find out when I returned at the end of the weekend. I took Monday off so I could go to the Amarillo Social Security Office. Dead there too—Mother, that is—but they said a doctor's letter could certify she was alive and possibly get the payments restored.

Six months later, after the letter and other attempts, the payments still hadn't been restored. Mercifully, an exterminator put an end to the mice, but not without warning me to never go close to the plastered hole where he had placed the deadly poison. At least now I could put my feet down when I made the endless phone inquiries to Social Security, even carrying my cell phone to class in case they called me back. After repeated calls to two different Social Security phone numbers, after several visits with varying documents to the Amarillo and the El Paso offices, after following different instructions from different offices, after getting certified to get access to Mother's records and thus act on her behalf (and this was not easy because she—legally deceased—had to sign for my right to do so; she signed, they still said she was dead)—all in the midst of my own doctor's appointments, self-help books, and deep breathing exercises—my friend Ani made a visit to Senator Sylvester Reyes's office. Ani's deceased husband, a lawyer, had a connection there, and she used it on my behalf. Within a week I had a letter and an apologetic call from someone in St. Louis: the Social Security payments would be restored, back payments made. It had been a clerical error. All this time the Medicare payments had lapsed too, with the hospital bills and group home costs mounting . . . "Go with the flow," Ani said. Don't resist.

But my mind buzzed more than ever with the "what ifs." There were a number of issues with the farm payments, the farm stock, the ins and outs of Mother's finances, whether or not to have the surgeries at her age, and how best to manage for her. Decisions, always decisions to be made. My brother seemed to be in denial about her real condition: He never came up to visit. He seemed unable to talk about anything serious on the phone. I know now he had his own problems, but then I was desperate.

I needed that big brother shoulder. Thankfully, Randy was there. But we never discussed personal things, except our mothers. The personal was there, but like a vapor exhaled into the serendipitous spaces of the Middle Alamosa. Without Randy, I could never have made all the hikes. He offered to take me back to one of the high places, this time east of the Middle Alamosa, to a place called Rotten Hill. It seemed an appropriate name, the way I was feeling. "Named according to the cowboys," he said. "No good for grazing." I wanted to see this place, which had a reputation for harboring Miocene dinosaur fossils. Randy and I put on our bloodhound faces, loaded the water, and headed up the old buffalo trail—now busy state Highway 385—to the ranch turnoff.

Rotten Hill is a mesa rising perhaps one hundred feet from the valley it dominates. Nearby Sierrita de la Cruz Creek—mostly dry of course—is the storied setting of fossil remains, pastores crossings, cowboy tales, and today's cattle ranching. Just that week, "something" had clawed to death a prize ranch mare in her stall. Cougar? Cougars supposedly had been extirpated from the Panhandle since the early twentieth century. Another mystery. The mesa shone red in the midday sun, a bright contrast with its Triassic ochre and purple shales and gravelly slopes to the aqua-blue sky. It was a stunning

Rotten Hill. *Author photo.*

assemblage of time passed. Marcy and Whipple had crossed south of here, steering by the largest permanent playa lake in the area locals call Milkweed. The creek itself was named because of an early-day sheepherder who planted a cross on a nearby hill. We stood at the bottom, puzzling over the best way up.

Randy bounded up, gazelle-like, straddling a slick drainage running from the mesa top to where we stood. More cautious, with my fragile knees, I took the slope diagonally and slower, enchanted by the many colors and shapes of the pebbled face. On the drive in, past the jagged fence posts grown up in the wet summer's grama and bear grass and rounding down into the valley veined with cattle trails and stunted juniper, I breathed in space. Up on top now, with views in all directions, space filled me. The day, its time and passing, the concerns of yesterday, disappeared. Even with my companion swishing ahead through the brush, stillness inhabited me. These continued trips into the breaks reminded me that internalized space experienced through time equals a sense of place. I'm home here.

We'd passed by sinkholes, warned by the landowner of the shifting clay bogs dotting the bottomland. We were closer here to the

Canadian than where I left off my summer hiking on the Middle Alamosa. Only a few miles away, the river terrain was a reminder of the uniqueness of each eco-area. I couldn't help it; I broke our trailblazing with a story.

"When I was a kid, there was no bridge over the Canadian River and we had to drive across the river to Tascosa. This meant crossing places where the water would get half-way up to the fender wells, and of course there were tales of people and horses being sucked down by the quick sand."

"Yeah," Randy echoed. "Don't you remember that Spanish armor that was recovered from the river years ago? Some Spanish conquistadores went down in the quicksand under that heavy load." We both nodded, knowing the armor rested as proof in the nearby Hereford, Texas, historical museum. Randy reminded me that his dad, also a lover of antiques, had kept the silver breastplate and shield at the hardware store until he donated it to the museum.

"My dad liked to start those kinds of stories about half-way to Tascosa, trying to scare us kids about the dangers of crossing the river," I continued. "I would hunker down lower and lower in the back seat, and by the time we actually crossed the river, I was hidden so I didn't have to look out and see us cross. The river was wide, just like it is today—clay bottom, sandy banks. Daddy would cry 'Here we go!' and gun the car across. The car would swerve this way and that like a carnival ride. I think I was too scared to squeal. I held my breath the whole time."

Dad's teasing was par for the course. This was the same man who would take us for a hamburger in Vega and then pretend he'd left his billfold at home. "Oh, I guess Shelley will have to wash the dishes," he would joke. I never did any dishes (the money recovered from deep in his pants pocket), so deep down I'd known we'd get across the Canadian somehow.

"Flint," Randy called over a bent shoulder. We examined what looks to be a campsite, charred surfaces, flint shards scattered around. Mostly Tecovas reds and purples. Here on the lip of the mesa, someone else prized space too. Why wouldn't the earlier inhabitants choose a high place to work—not just for refuge but for the sheer beauty of the place itself?

Near the scattered flint, we found cobbles and what looked to be tepee rings. Could this have been a camp of Kiowa or Comanche? Randy mentioned he knew of a flint quarry nearby, so their flint-knapping used localized jasper, not the dolomite from the Alibates quarry sixty miles east. The rainbow of rocks—from the red creek bottom to the slope striations called "Spanish skirts" for their multicolor, like the ruffled costume of dancers—created a synesthesia for me. A kind of throbbing of the spirit comes from the colors, as if they have energy. Though vibrating, they feel like peace. I often had this sensation at the farm where even the drought's harshness would soften and glow around dusk. I glowed too.

Maybe it was the humidity or the altitude. The light in New Mexico, I knew, was celebrated for its clarity, an aesthetic intensity drawing artists and writers. Why is there no poet of the plains? Perhaps it's because few lingered, stayed long enough to be filled with the translucence of stillness. For here it's not the "clear, bright, harsh, almost blinding field of view," as Robert Coles characterizes New Mexico light, but the "hazy, somewhat softened, even blurred vision" of the plains. Land of mirages, of imagination.

We know Native peoples historically have sought high places, often for vision quests. Manuel García Rejón, in his Comanche dictionary, translated by Dan Gelo, notes that the word *piacane*, "mountain," also translates into "Comanche temple." And the Comanche had a name for the essence of colors. Places and their colors could be power places. Red represented earth power; yellow, sun power; and green, the power of regenerative life. Canyon edges could thus be places of power—the overlooks—but also because of their cliffs and canyons (earth), caprock badlands (yellow), and the dappling of cottonwoods and junipers (green) nearby, possibly signaling water sources.

Can a contemporary person experience the powers of place? Gelo believes that Comanche sacred places were power places but not so much for the place itself, but for what took place there. The universal spirit wells up in such a place but is available only to the sensitive person who may be receptive to it.

I remembered again what the elder of the White Mountain Apache said about "wisdom sits in places": "It's like water that never dries up. Well, you also need to drink from places. You must remember everything about them. You must learn their names. You must remember what happened at them long ago. You must think about it and keep on thinking about it. Then your mind will become smoother and smoother. You will walk a long way and live a long time. You will be wise. People will respect you." Omnivorous Wolf River, as the Comanche called you. Your name warns us of your hunger—silver shields, men and horses. Tributary Atascosa Creek—boggy bottom—there are sink holes nearby.

I doubted the part about being wise and respected, in our world, that is. And I wondered about the word "power," which for me had some negative connotations. But power is energy, the realization that place is powerful, again according to the Comanche, in that it is a place to meet the power donors, animals like bears, eagles, wolves. As with the Comanche and the Kiowa, we had pushed the bear and the wolf from the Panhandle. Eagles remained a rare sight.

That summer I had seen a circling of hawks, northern harriers, I think. Not eagles, but graceful, falcon-like, pale with unbarred black tail. There had been a number coasting around; I had noticed them before. But suddenly, just off the access road to the farm, I saw a large number of them kiting up and down, acrobatic despite their adult-size three-foot wingspan. Closer, they seemed in turmoil. Then I saw: they were looping up and down, passing a rabbit among them. Over and over again in the circles of motion the rabbit slipped from one swooping set of claws to another. It looked like a game. A high-wire act. But then I laughed at my silly perception. They were likely not sharing the cottontail but fighting over it. Whatever: it was a beautiful riot.

If we no longer had the top predators as power donors, would their underlings do? Randy and I mustered on, and I took to following the game trails up on top of the mesa. Deer certainly, maybe coyote, a skunk. I hoped for a bobcat, or even better, cougar tracks. I stepped alongside the tracks—such encounters had always been special, like being anointed, a blessing. I doubted I absorbed the heart of an antelope when I returned his stare, or the cold intelligence of a prairie rattler I almost stepped on. But the other day when I crawled under a barbed wire fence and found myself eye to eye with a horned toad, frozen, camouflaged in place, I learned a bit about power and the humility to receive it. I blinked before he did and eased away.

Like the Indians say, we've lost the talent of talking to animals. But they're still talking. Randy and I pulled up beside the ranch horses, rub their noses, exchange the day's events. We called out to the mother cows balking in the road. And when I'm alone, I do, I talk to the animals.

Back in El Paso to my job, another loop, another circle—back and forth, back and forth, juggling this and that—I tried to sustain the unutterable natural world in the noisy, red-message-light-on-your-phone city. Of course, I loved my teaching, particularly my students, working with literature and culture, a "job" in which you were always learning. I was teaching an honors course in environmental writing, renting a concrete block house out on a cactus-covered escarpment a few miles out from El Paso to get in the mood. Mornings and evenings were stunning—the Franklin Mountains, the worn down southern end of the Rockies, rising in the eastern sky. Though this was the Chihuahuan Desert and not the plains, the area shared much with the llano and its canyons: some of the same plant life and a history of ancient seas. And the Mogollon had been here possibly, traders with the Antelope Creek people. One morning there was fog in the farming valley, so much so that it looked like an ocean. Two bare peaks barely showed from the Franklins and immediately I was struck by how similar the landscape of that moment was to the ocean view off Lanikai near Kailua Hawai'i where I'd lived. There two small cone-shaped islands pierced the azure sea. I had no photograph, only my memory to reckon the connection. Llano to desert to ocean. Continuities where there had seemed only fragmentations.

So here was the arc of the story.

I had seen it from Landergin, one magical late afternoon when a rainstorm over the Canadian left a faint rainbow in the far sky. Mary Austin used that image to describe the seamless genius of being of the Pueblo people. She imagined this arc also as a "sacred middle"— the "middle ground between art and knowledge"—native knowledge, that is: "the voiceless passion of spirit toward form . . . the ever living and as yet uncreated Life, pressing to be shaped into tree and shrub . . . the grass to be man." Breaking with the conventional Western metaphorical thinking, she described "being" instead. That long view toward Ysabel's Camp reminded me that I sought some connection between my dad's life and Ysabel's—between Armitage Farms, where I started my walk toward the Canadian, and Ysabel's adobe house, where I would end.

But that was not all.

Interviewed for a WPA project, an old sheepherder of Ysabel's day recounted an exchange with a Comanche who confirmed his people had camped on Landergin Mesa. Despite the artifacts of the Antelope Creek people, he insisted his people were the first and the only (such a human trait). Yet here in oral story and shared memory was a bridge between the 1930s and the 1700s and then, with the Antelope Creek people, to the 1200s. And the Antelope Creek people themselves left clues to their connection to a Woodland people whose existence in the Panhandle dates from 400 A.D. Today's Pawnee hold a cultural memory of people from the Southwest arriving and integrating into their tribe. The Skidi Pawnee were early-day astronomers, basing their origin narrative and other beliefs on the closely watched heavens. Records show that the Antelope Creek people—who possibly migrated out of the Panhandle, eventually integrating with the Pawnee—created at least one site where astrological knowledge could have held sway. At the Footprint site, near Lake Meredith, one of the many Antelope Creek Phase sites along the Canadian, large footprints were etched in the basalt along with nodules arranged in the shape of what could indicate constellations in the night sky. And a mirror of this stone configuration occurs at a Mogollon site in Arizona. Such fragile and complex links suggest not only continuity from Dad's to Ysabel's but with all that lies in between. Middle Alamosa, where water is mostly a memory, we still drink from your places.

Leaving Rotten Hill, Randy and I got lost. We'd dawdled like misbehaving twins in a Pueblo myth and paid the price by taking this road and that into the night. Ranch roads make little sense after dark. We were out of water; Randy's cell phone wouldn't work out here. To me, the worst thing that could happen was that we'd have to spend the night in the pickup, then find our way in the morning. But then again, this wasn't good. Randy's girlfriend would worry if he's not home, as would my partner miles away. The sheriff might be called out to find us. People would talk. They probably already were:

older lady, younger man, always headed north into the country. We had lingered at the flint site, totally absorbed with the mother lode of Tecovas, probably mined by the point makers atop Rotten Hill. Like bandits we'd loaded whole, beautifully striated chunks into Randy's truck. We both had rock gardens at home. The gods weren't happy. The truck was running out of gas.

I thought of the Antelope Creek and the Skidi Pawnee too, how their night sky knowledge would bring them home. I wondered what lying atop Landergin this night rather than the cramped cab of a pickup would show us. Then, two anxious hours into our fright we caught a road that looked familiar. We skidded back into Vega on empty.

↓ I thought I could see the end of the story too, in that arc, even before getting there. On my phone there was a message from James at the group home. It was late but I called. James did most of the talking. Mother required hospice. I needed to come in before I left and sign some papers, consult with the hospice doctor.

I read where one of the Lakota chiefs spoke to his people before their lands were taken away. "Look upon these lands with care," he admonished. "Memorize them, hold them dear. Your memory will keep them close—only this will last because the land itself will be taken away." *Yes, yes.*

Back in my Vega house, I packed to go and remembered something I had written in my journal of an earlier August. Shored up in my notebook—holding one of those memories:

> Thinking about the circles, the tipi rings of the Comanche, the sacred circles. Mary Austin, writing about the Indians she knew, talking about the circling of the "sacred middle." And then out in the yard, for the last watering, I see the monarch butterflies that migrate through here to Mexico. They come each year, in the time of the sunflowers, just before school begins. Their larvae feed on the milkweeds in the pastures, they are attracted to smells, the fruit rotting on my apple tree. They like the sound of running water. I walk among the trees, their orange delight crowning me with elliptical joy.

CHAPTER FIVE

Rocks and Remnants

I danced and danced, turning in circles Sufi-like (had I known of Sufis), knocking up against the coats, sliding over the pine floor. From the dance hall came "Cotton-Eye Joe" and other old favorites. The adults were out there square dancing. Somewhere my parents lined up in an obedient row.

"You're coming with us, tonight, Punkin," my dad had humored. Roy got to do something fun, like go over to his friend's house, maybe spend the night. I had to go with Mother and Daddy to the "square" dance.

My dad was a caller. He called some of the dances like "Take your partner, do-si-do," and when my parents danced—Mother in her squaw dress of crepe and colorful rickrack, circular skirt so large it dragged the floor when she sewed the ruffles on her sewing machine, and Daddy in his western shirt and oval belt buckle—they were a dashing couple. My balding daddy was upright and tall and graceful, smooth in his movements yet strong. He spun Mother, a petite five feet and bright eyed, as if she clung to his belt buckle. Even though I sometimes felt odd-man out, I could see how much my parents loved each other, the fun they had no matter what they seemed to be doing, and I was happy. There was a settling grace about them.

But as the youngest kid of older parents I was often alone at adult gatherings, and so tonight my partner was a straight-backed broomstick. I had rescued it from its fate—cleaning up after the dance—by wrenching the pole loose from the broom end. I unwound a coat hanger, straightening out the wire as best I could, wrapped the wire around the pole, and made two arms. Broom and I danced and danced, but I must admit I felt I always had the lead.

My mother made me a squaw dress, a vivid turquoise with rounds of rickrack on the completely circular skirt. I had spun in that too. And my dad tried to teach me to dance. When we two-stepped I felt a hesitation, a kind of unanticipated dip in his movements, which threw me off the rhythm. Like a good jazz player, I thought, he dropped a beat, but not on purpose. How was it my parents looked so perfect together, yet I felt I couldn't follow his lead? He dipped when I lurched on. I took deep breaths. We started over.

I liked whirling with Broom because there was no beginning or end to it, no pressure or expectations. I felt free in the mindless rhythm of something beyond the music of western swing. I never did much like western music anyway. I preferred Elvis Presley, my brother's rhythm and blues 45s, and Peter and the Wolf.

⇓ Mother sat across the room, silent, staring at something that was not exactly the television. I was uncomfortable again, discussing her condition with the hospice doctor who insisted on talking to me and about her as if she were an object. With Mother's permission, given when she had been mentally competent, I had long ago signed the Do Not Resuscitate directive. But now the hospice documents were a different thing altogether.

"Don't worry," he was saying. But his words were no comfort. "She'll be comfortable. She'll likely lose all her faculties. Virtually starve to death. But she won't suffer."

I flashed to what our friend Mildred said about the death of her mother for whom she denied medical intervention—a feeding tube mainly. Carrie was shutting down, as they say, and though Mildred knew it, knew this was the kindest way, she always felt guilty. "I starved my mother to death," she said.

The doctor was so matter of fact. I guess I thought he would check Mother, refer to her records, ask more questions. Instead, he seemed to follow a writ. He never glanced her way. *Don't worry. She'll starve to death. But she won't suffer.*

"The body just shuts down under these circumstances, naturally," he added, but I hardly heard him. My ears were ringing as my blood pressure rose again.

Just two weeks before, I'd been teasing with my mother. I had her large Magnavox television moved from her house (and from care facility to care facility), as if its familiarity would seem like an old friend accompanying her from place to place. We hooked up a VCR, like she had back at her house, so I could show her the movies she so loved. How much of any show Mother could follow was unknown, but she seemed to focus intently and respond to the movies, news, and yes, advertisements. My mother must have inspired the "shop until you drop" moniker. When I was a kid she'd drag me from store to store Saturdays. As she tried on what seemed to me to be an endless stream of outfits (and shopped for Dad and me too) I would slip under the coat racks that lined the walls and fall asleep. To this day clothing stores make me sleepy.

I had a VCR tape of myself as a baby and another of Roy and his first birthday cake. My parents were inveterate film nuts. They made photographs or film of family events with every generation of camera (and every generation of family). One of Dad's hobbies was running the 16-mm camera and projector. He had a splicing kit and took the final product seriously. I never knew whether it was the endless array of birthday cakes as subject or their fascination with film itself, but our family had a faithful record of birthdays, anniversaries, parties, and rites of passage, like my first day of school and when my brother got his first car. In one of their first films I stroll toward the school steps, dressed in checked pinafore and saddle oxfords, trying to look casual and detached—hands decorously positioned behind my back. I pause, cast a serious but nonchalant look over my shoulder, and enter the building.

Today I dusted off a tape to bring to the group home. Converted from one of the early 16-mm films, it captured the day my parents picked me up from the Volunteers of America adoption home. We all liked to celebrate this day I was "chosen" by my parents. This was our epic journey: like Moses and the bulrushes, a wonderful family had rescued me from an alternate journey that could have ended up who knows where? In fact, just two weeks after my parents accepted my adoption (after a two-year wait), another agency they were registered with contacted them. They told me, *You were chosen.* And they felt they had been chosen too.

When she was at the Walton's, the group home, I asked my mother if she minded if I tried to find my birth mother and perhaps father. I'm not sure she was paying full attention when she nodded "yes," but I began to research Volunteers of America, the agency from which I was adopted. They had since discontinued this service, but the adoption records were with the State of Texas. Following the law, I petitioned the appropriate district court for an intermediary who would represent both the anonymous birth child and the birth mother whom she sought to contact. When I received the records from the state, I found that my name and hers were redacted throughout. The bold black lines expunging pertinent private information made me want to do an art installation of them, lining the walls with omissions and gaps, searching as in a Morse code for a pattern. . . .——-—. . . The most fascinating part was a record of the social worker's interview with her before my birth. She was asked if she had Native American blood, I'm assuming due to her looks. (I found this ironic since my adoptive mother did have Native ancestors.) I wrote her at the address of the intermediary: *Dear Birth Mother.* . . . She wrote one purple note paper letter back. But that was it. Understandably, she didn't want to reveal her identity or place of residence, nor did she want to meet me. But it was enough to know I had been a love child and also a child loved.

Daddy did the filming. The maybe sixty-second film features bald-headed-baby-me, six weeks old, and Mother. Dressed smartly in a green suit with a pert feather-tipped hat, she holds me tenderly in her arms as she seems to waltz from the two-story home for unwed mothers (which appeared to be out in the country) and scoots into the Chevy coop.

Cut. That was it. At the group home we played it over and over. Felix, one of the group home caregivers, was transfixed and wanted to see it again and again. It was like an origin myth.

I think of this now. How we celebrated the details in these amateur remains (the fragile original film could break at any moment), like the stare of someone from the upper story windows—one of the unwed mothers at the home (was she mine?), looking down. How I wanted to rewind it one more time, take us back, restore the beginnings, see that face, both my mothers' faces, before we all fade out.

⋎ Randy and I stood in the bend of the Middle Alamosa maybe a mile from Battleship Mesa, another locally named butte, the final dramatic landmark before the Middle Alamosa breaks away into the flat, pebbled reddening run to the Canadian. We were at Espendiza Windmill, a site indicated on some maps. We had come here before, late in a day when we couldn't continue. We dangled our legs over the cliffside then, marveling at the sunset, eating our roast beef sandwiches. Today we had hats and water and an early start on what was proving to be a tough landscape, full of thick prickly pear cactus and dense stands of mesquite.

The land looked blighted. Dry, overgrazed. Except for the windmill, which was in good shape, it was a place abandoned to itself. A road led raggedly, weaving between taller cottonwoods and overgrown bushes, scratching the pickup as we drove to the windmill and dead-ended there. We would leave the truck and walk. It was always easiest just to follow the Middle Alamosa creek bed.

Randy's days were bookended by work at the hardware store and now his own mother's needs. Like mine, his dad had died years before, and because he was the sibling returned to Vega ("just for a stop in, just for a month or two"), Shirley's care fell to him.

"Can't be gone too long," he explained. "The mother thing."

I was sympathetic but I wanted us still to be beyond the ring of cell phones, the messages that followed us everywhere. I didn't remind him he probably couldn't get calls out here. When we headed back evenings he always whipped out his phone first high place we crested. He wanted to know. I didn't.

Here was yet another spectacularly wide and looping depression shaped by the Middle Alamosa for countless years. I found myself wondering what this site looked like to the Antelope Creek people, what the riverbed and bluffs were like, what plants sustained them. Pollen research turned up mostly native plants: sunflowers, yucca, soapberry, hackberry, mesquite, plums, cattail stems, persimmons, prickly pear, purslane, goosefoot, grass seeds. Despite the continued erosion and geologic changes, the landscape we walked sustained the same plants as those known to the Antelope Creek people. But they had apparently also grown corn, squash, and beans. The bone remains of mammals revealed pervasive crushing. Everything had been used, down to the oil and grease it could produce.

But what of these plant people? The farmer in me appreciated their essential knowledge of plants, a supplement necessary for the Plains Indians as well as the hunter / agriculturalists. I surveyed the dry conditions and clayey soils the nearer we got to the Canadian and recalled that Dr. J. M. Bigelow, serving as official botanist for the Whipple reconnaissance, had recognized the potential of the prairie grasses: "Many of our farmers wish to introduce the culture of these grasses at home," he reported, because they retained their nutrients the year round. "But it is to be presumed . . . they are only well adapted to arid climates." Even if they were overgrazed, the short-grass prairie grasses have persisted through the climate changes known to human time. I could identify them by now—buffalo grass, various gramas, sacaton, little bluestem, needle-and-thread. As we entered yet another drought cycle, I marveled at their staying power. And ours. After all we feed upon these grasses, even as all matter of consuming creatures—mammals, birds, even insects—feed us.

So grass, as well as forbs, woody plants, seeds, fed an observant and respectful people. Accounts confirm that indigenous people in general not only excelled at plant usage but celebrated plants in ceremony and prayer. The Kiowa and Comanche were excellent botanists, as plant gathering for food, ceremony, and medicine supplemented their primarily buffalo diet. The Antelope Creek people gathered but also propagated plants, occasionally building terraces close to the river—for example at Saddleback Mountain east of the Middle Alamosa—in order to raise their food. The complaints of dry land farmers seemed nothing to me as I looked at the places these villagers attempted to crop.

They must have talked to the plants too. The record of one Native American ecology recounts how two desert dwelling people, the Navajo and the Apache, related to plants. One Navajo reported, "You must ask permission of the plant [to pick it] or the medicine won't work. . . . Plants are alive; you must give them a good talk." The Apaches spoke of yucca and other plants as their "brothers" and "sisters." Prayers and offerings were given. Plains tribes celebrated the forked cottonwood, which would serve as the central pole in the Sun Dance lodge. I imagined the ceremonial power of both the tree and the buffalo skull mounted on it for the Sun Dance: animal and plant and people linked in this regenerative celebration.

As I looked at the dense cacti and mesquite flatlands near the Middle Alamosa, I found it amazing that approximately one hundred indigenous species representing thirty-nine plant families here had some potential for economic or medicinal importance for the prehistoric people in the region. Picking your way between the cactus plants you must look down, and only then do you begin to see the diversity. In this area too thick for bison—and now cattle—to browse, the careful gatherer would be rewarded with yucca, cedar, buckwheat, hackberry, and Indian mallow.

I was beginning to see the richness of what appeared derelict when Randy waved me over. He had bushwhacked ahead and was pointing toward a flat-topped, freestanding mesa rising in the distance. Conical like Landergin, the mesa seemed to appear and disappear, depending on the brush cover and our approach, as if it were dodging us.

We'd come out of the creek bed, deep in mudstone and clays. It's another world there down within the Pleistocene walls sure to hold some mammoth's tooth, some Miocene remnant. From this distinct area of massive, deeply eroded switchbacks, the freestanding mesa ahead looks foreign, displaced. Up top, we walked maybe a half mile and—like the scrub juniper area south of Paint Rock near a dry playa lake that revealed an immature great horned owl seeming to play hide-and-seek behind branches—the mesa teases us with its grey mirage.

As we came closer and the mesa loomed taller, the soil near it now bare of any grass or shrub, a fine shale and chalk slowed our daylong plodding. I stopped in a field of boulders and looked around. Randy had disappeared—all but his cowboy hat—into a telltale tributary cut to the Middle Alamosa. Puckered sandstone, now furled one ridge upon another, signaled a dried spring's presence. The ground was so bleached we felt its reflection even in late afternoon.

"Not Landergin, but a lot like it," he offered.

"Yes, I'm wondering how this lines up with Landergin and Little Arrowhead. Gotta be one of those hunting sites or even settlements. Maybe all three functioned at the same time."

"Wonder if we can climb it?"

"No way."

At bottom we agreed. The parched shale, faded to pale greys, was like gritty tumblers under our shoes. We slipped this way and that just on the slopes but climbed as high as we could, looking for artifacts. We began to circle the bottom, noting the eroded top and displaced boulders; something might show up here below. As we rounded the circular mesa bottom, two similarly shaped freestanding mesas revealed themselves north. Three mesas, then. We marveled. Creek and springs have shaped these pyramid-like fortresses leaving a valley of rocks.

"You know what I read about Landergin?" I said to Randy.

"What now?" He teases me because I rush home after jaunts to research and read up on where we've been, what we've seen.

"Well, the stone they used to make their houses had to be gotten from the sandstone top where they lived. So they literally took stone from the edges, probably, through time, essentially building on a foundation they were slowly destroying."

"Sounds familiar. Like present-day sand and gravel pits and oil sites on this ranch, destroying the very riches they benefit from. Are these mesas on any map you've seen?"

I said no, but then once home consulted the one archaeological reconnaissance done on the Middle Alamosa Creek, in 1972. Individual sites, some forty-four recorded in all, were indicated by a numbering system, and when I read through the sites, the only one named was Landergin. Everything else had a number, even Little Arrowhead. It took some time, but finally I located a two-paragraph summary that I thought summarized the mesas we discovered. It described abundant lithic and ceramic materials at the summit and on the slopes and noted the cultural affiliation as Panhandle Aspect, with possible Archaic representation.

The archaeological team had climbed this mesa, finding eighteen shards of Borger cord-marked pottery with angular quartz temper, along with Fresno and Ellis projectile points. The report's mention of Panhandle Aspect (meaning Woodland or later Antelope Creek characteristics) could suggest a date of occupation anywhere from 0 to 1500 A.D. The Archaic assumption would date occupation much earlier, from 4000 B.C. to the time of Christ. These people had been bison hunters but also seed gatherers.

Roy R. Armitage in Vega. *Author photo.*

Later on the phone, Randy said just one thing about the mesas: "We've got to name them."

⌄ My brother, Roy, came to see Mother. Doris at the group home had phoned him (a surprise to me), urging him to see her, trying to explain her rapidly failing health. I was relieved but also nervous. "Entertaining" Roy was not hard, but the guilt, unnecessary, unexplained, ran deep. He wasn't as close to Mother as I—and I never could quite come up with a satisfactory explanation. Somehow he seemed to think she wasn't as close to him either.

It could have been the farm stock, but it had to go farther back than that. Years before my dad had made the farm a corporation, its value measured in stock. When she was still cogent Mother had signed over 55 percent of the farm to me, 45 percent to Roy. Her lawyer advised that someone actually had to run the farm, so one of us needed "controlling interest." I had been involved through the years; he had not. I knew the farm business, and although the few times Roy came he donned his western shirts, hats, and boots and played cowboy and rancher for the weekend, he wasn't up on the farm business. His memories were of tractors driving themselves and Jimmy collaborations, not of agribusiness that required frequent exchanges with the local Farm Security Administration folks. He was there. I was (part of the time, but consistently) here. Mother and I had operated the farm after Daddy's death. He had been in Omaha, Nebraska, working at his job with Northern Natural Gas. Of course he was *capable* of doing it, but he was just too far away.

But there was an unspoken unease. Mother had begun her letter of stock allocation with "I love you both dearly." And she certainly did. At the advice of her lawyer, Mother gave me controlling interest because I was able and willing to come take care of the farm. My parents had never favored one child over the other. For Roy, I feared, this decision was but another sediment of crusted-over ill will. A few people in Vega thought Mother and Daddy spoiled Roy as a child—and why not? They lost their first son, a premie, at birth. They continued their generosity into Roy's adulthood. But when my father died, something changed. Roy and his wife Sue had the responsibilities and demands of children and grandchildren. They had cared for Sue's parents too. On one occasion when my mother went to Katy for Christmas, she gave her grandsons and her eldest grandson's daughters each one hundred dollars in their Christmas cards. When James, Roy's youngest son, opened his card, somehow the money wasn't there. Rather than view this as a mistake—or guess that the money had slipped out somehow—they blamed Mother, as if she had purposely favored one over the other. Perhaps the resentments and assumptions trickled up and down. Roy was caught in the middle; Mother felt that too.

I watched most of this family drama from the sidelines, absorbing the hurts and trying to play peacemaker. The little sis who came along nine years later than Roy, I had been dearly loved by my big brother and often felt I had to make up for the disappointments on both sides. Roy and some members of his family sometimes appeared put off by Mother, which put me sadly and awkwardly in the middle of a fray that was palpable but unarticulated.

And now Roy was here. "She doesn't know me," he said.

Mother had taken to staring, but she would squeeze your hand or touch your sleeve. She knew.

Roy sat with her all day, dutifully, sweetly. But he expected more. "No, she doesn't say anything. She hasn't talked to me."

"Roy, look," I said already raising my voice, though trying to keep the shrill past at bay. "She hasn't been able to talk in months. She doesn't talk to me or anyone. She can't. But she knows you are here. You can see it in her eyes."

Mother's eyes lighted up when Roy first arrived. I knew she was happy he was there. When they sat there together I could see the resemblance: the fine-boned features, the angular faces, unusual eyes. Roy had golden eyes, ochre like the Trujillo shales; Mother's now were post-cataract blue, but they still shone with an inner knowing and sometimes an impish humor. Most people thought Roy took after my dad's side of the family; he had those Armitage ears. His nickname in high school was "Rabbit." But he had the Dunns' good looks: curly blonde hair when he was younger, a chiseled face, fine nose. The Christmas cards Mother and Daddy had made from photographs when we were young showed a Hollywood-gorgeous little boy.

Today he's still snappy in his crisply ironed western shirt. "I'm going to Cavender's to check out some new boots. I shouldn't buy them," he trailed off, ready to take a shopping break. Roy also liked to shop. Despite his complaints about the cost of the trip, he brought a brand-new, top-of-the-line Dell portable computer in tow. And later, the boots. And a couple of new western shirts. He liked the gadgets and the smart things, my Roy.

How I'd missed my big brother. And not just for shouldering the burdens of decision making for our mother. I missed his goofy humor, his loping stride, and when he wasn't distracted by what he often alluded to as financial and family worries, his love of life. Roy was a people person—an EMT, a volunteer fireman—like my dad, a civic-minded person who also deeply valued his friends. A fine family man. But I felt a distance from me, his little sis.

I tried telling him about my hikes in the breaks, about the connection of Armitage Farms to the Canadian River history. He looked at

Rocky Middle Alamosa Creek bed near East Prong Windmill. *Author photo.*

a photo or two and said he wanted to check out the NASCAR on the television. He was preoccupied. He loved fast cars, country-western music, and slightly to the right politics. I gave him a check, on the farm, to cover his airfare. He never asked about the farm.

⋎ Randy and I laughed at our bulging pockets. Rocks here, rocks there. "I've almost ruined my washer," he said. Flint, stones clogging up the filter.

"At least you have a washer and dryer," I joked. My house had neither.

"And you've got enough rocks in your pockets to keep from blowing away," he added.

What was the attraction to the rocks? We started every trip to the breaks with our heads down, searching for that unusual shape, that striking color—whatever struck our eye. When we showed a new prize to each other, we couldn't explain. Mostly we returned the stones to their places in the configuration of things, but each of us also had a prominent rock garden at home. And in my case, I had a considerable collection inside as well. Thumb-sized "guitar pic" scrapers, large hand-held ones, bird points, arrowheads, hammer stones. I identified them on back, "Landergin Mesa—top," "Pioneer Hill—Green's." Even Armitage Farms was a source: for a one-inch long Alibates white with a light brown striation. One day I found a Tecovas reworked point as I walked the pasture that surrounds my house in Vega, reminding me that old Indian trails likely passed here, later followed by Whipple and Marcy. Following our archaeologist friend's caution we never dug or disturbed a site, and surface shards we documented on back with time and location.

Maybe I came by my fascination with rocks naturally. I told a friend of my great aunt's, "No, they weren't your usual spoon aunts," referring to the collections older women might favor. "One was a book aunt. Another a story-telling aunt. And the third, my Aunt Reita, a rock aunt." Married to a geologist and both of them lovers of the outdoors and collecting, Aunt Reita had rooms that were a stumped toe waiting to happen. Each door was propped open with a large geode. Other rocks appeared in the hallway, on the stairway. Meteorite pieces decorated the dining table. A butterfly cut of delicate pink Iowa pine coral graced a bedroom chest of drawers.

And then there was my high school biology teacher who was forever challenging us to learn something new. One day he passed around a large oblong stone with obvious phallic connotations. "Lick it," he commanded, "See how your tongue sticks to it." To this day I think these were honest instructions made toward a miniature lesson in geology. We snickered and turned up our noses. The rock made its way around the room, each of us choosing a hopefully "clean" spot for our experiment. When it came back to his desk, he said: "Now, this is petrified dinosaur dung." I doubt that was true, but he made some point about rock texture, density, composition, age. Interested in fossils and dinosaurs and the like since childhood, I really didn't mind. It tasted pretty good.

Those dog-eared pages from *The World We Live In*—particularly the ones with the dinosaurs—convinced me by fourth grade I wanted to be a paleontologist. After our earlier trip to Rotten Hill, I was going back through my pockets and discovered an elliptical nodule shaped "stone" which shone like agate and looked petrified. I called up Carolyn Richardson, wife of one of the infamous arrowhead hunters in Oldham County, the one honored with the mock monument atop

Landergin Mesa, the now deceased Ralph Slutz. Could I come over and look at his collections? I had something in my pocket I wanted to ask her about.

Carolyn's house is the old Doc Lloyd house in Vega. Doc was one of the early settlers and an early physician in Vega. His office was in his house. Slutz had bought the house from the Lloyd estate in the 1950s, and Carolyn's second husband, Wayne Richardson (also deceased), most recently had updated it with a concrete wrap-around porch where the wooden one had decayed and new siding mimicking wood. As I approached the house it was still imposing, its two story Colonial style once a showpiece in this small town. I remembered going see Doc Lloyd there, dreading the appointment, but wide-eyed once inside where the fifteen-foot ceilings, fainting couches, and rich wood baseboards and banisters expanded my already Poe-like imagination. Doc had a reputation for miracle cures and had once broken the fever of a sick man by packing him in ice in the clawfoot bathtub. It is definitely a house fit for surprises and dark secrets. Today, as Carolyn, graying curls brightened by her ever-present purple pant outfits and matching costume jewelry, met me at the door, I expected some.

"Here they are," she said, her elliptical matching purple earrings dancing. We entered the spacious living room, which still seemed large to me although every crack and cranny was filled.

She pointed to the wall where three picture frames hung, full of scores of spear, arrow, and dart points. Leaning over the couch where they hung to get a better look, I saw Ralph had been drawn to the tiniest, most delicate points. I asked where he had collected these.

"All over," she said. "From childhood on, he would walk all the way to the river." The Slutzes had land out north, bordering the Green ranch. I imagined Ralph striking out, following his whims. The sleuthing continued into his advanced age.

"He had a knack for seeing the flint," she added. "Some people can, some can't."

"To think about human hands fashioning these maybe thousands of years ago," I said, as much to myself as Carolyn. It was a pedestrian comment, but I marveled at the Clovis and Folsom points—large, lightly fluted, gray spear points that, according to archaeologists, date from the Ice Age. Some of the pieces were of

Alibates flint, confirming that the quarry site had been in use at least thirteen thousand years.

"But look at these." Carolyn pointed to cases hung adjacent to Ralph's collection.

Randy told me that Carolyn had found "dinosaur" teeth and bones out on Baca's Ranch near Rotten Hill years ago. And here they were. She had framed the remains of two creatures. One resembled a large and ferocious looking horny toad with spikes along the sides and back, *Desmatosuchus haplocerus*. A drawing was mounted alongside the other fossil—*Buettneria perfecta*—illustrating a meat-eater, approximately six feet long or more, a shovel-headed amphibian that had survived from the Devonian era into the Jurassic. Carolyn was the local librarian and amateur historian (I later observed in her bathroom stacks of plastic storage boxes full of Oldham County memorabilia, including one labeled "Ed Murphy") and was an apt researcher. From sources and interviews with regional university archaeologists, she found that this amphibian had a crocodile-like head and likely moved upon land with a similar locomotion.

"I'm not good at finding flint," Carolyn said. Dinosaur bones fascinated her more.

"Where did you find these?" I knew but wanted to hear it from Carolyn.

"Rotten Hill."

I remembered how Randy, Lisa Jackson, and Jeff Indeck, the Panhandle-Plains Historical Museum curator, and I had set out one day on Baca's Ranch to reconnoiter the only archaeologically documented site for these creatures. The Panhandle preserves the most dynamic and comprehensive record of Miocene fossils in the country, Jeff told us as we trekked through the small pocked field of stones he said were geodes, past Tecovas cliffs, until Lisa faltered in the hot August sun. Waiting for Lisa to recover, we scoured the area, examined rocks. One of them rested in my pocket. We never made it to the site. But here I was standing before what we'd sought.

"What are those?" I pointed to yet a third hanging display between Ralph's points and Carolyn's fossils.

"Oh, those are the teeth we found of the horny toad–looking creature."

"But did you have them polished? They look like agate."

"No, this is just how they were—are."

I fingered the question I had lingering in my pocket, rolled it between my fingers, then showed Carolyn.

The long oval "stone" with its layers of brown striations was a match to Carolyn's recovered dinosaur teeth.

"I thought it was agate . . ." I trailed off, obviously still not able to identify my rocks.

"Where did you find it?"

"Rotten Hill." I felt again the strange entanglement of stone's element.

My friend Peggy Church spent a considerable time pondering stones. She wrote at least fourteen poems on that subject from 1923 to 1981. I like to reread them after hiking. Like my Aunt Reita who collected rock specimens and was married to a geologist, Peggy (also married to a geologist) melded her poet's sensitivity to scientific knowledge. She wrote about stones' transformative power and, despite our notion that they are inanimate, their living natures. In "Stones on an Arid Hillside," she likens the markings on stones to grooves of music, audible if we only knew the right key, "the correct equation." "Would [their] colors be audible?" she asks; could "the stones call out to one another?" "If I could listen," she concludes, "would I someday hear the stone's voice / that goes on and on putting God into its own voice?"

⅄ "We'll name them Dorothy Mae and Shirley," Randy said, pushing what I felt was a small flint shard into my pocket. Mother's funeral. People coming and going in the foyer before the service. I am distracted by his attention.

"What?"

"The mesas. We'll name them Shirley and Dorothy Mae."

⅄ Like Medicine Mounds, on the south bank of the Red River below Palo Duro, southeast of the Middle Alamosa, landform names for the Comanche reveal ecological relationships, that "sacred motion" connecting all beings. Some iron meteorites Comanches venerated for their ability to "speak." There are records of the Comanche visiting this site to strike the rock with a drumstick or lance; the rock spoke in its ringing and vibration. *I'm listening.*

Deep Canyon cut of the Middle Alamosa Creek. *Author photo.*

⅄ Roy is leaving, and I go one last time to say goodbye, too, to Mother. I'm driving back to El Paso that Sunday afternoon. She reclines in her chair—that stare—but blinks and nods when he bends to lightly kiss her on the cheek. For just that moment I see that tender brother beneath the layers of time, the influences of others, the separations, the distances. I hug him at the door, and then decide to go back to tell Mother goodbye one more time. But something has shifted, something changed. Her eyes seem to have turned backward in her head. "Mother, Mother," I say waiting for some tiny movement, some bare squeeze of recognition. I wait. She has waited. For Roy. Then she could let go. In the awful silence, I see my mother finally has turned to stone.

"History for the Comanches," as historian Daniel Flores writes in his *Alternate Worlds: Comanche Sense of Place and the Pre-Agricultural Llano Estado,* "did not evolve progressively forward but rather cycled backward, via ritual, and sacred spaces, to mythological time. Dance ritual was the principal technique for re-creating the mythological past." In dance, another sacred motion, they acknowledged movements and relationships between humans and places—according to Flores "to gain inner peace from the acceptance of full human participation in the wondrous cycle of birth, growth, death, a circle that one witnesses."

⋁ Randy and I return to the mesas by the creek bottom. We pass a high cliff and comment on the singular beauty of the cliff rose—some roots exposed, but clinging, almost suspended in air, atop the escarpment. On our return, coming back the same way, we are surprised to see that a side of the channel we crossed only moments before—and the rose with it—has crashed to the ground, exposing mesquite roots that now dangle. How strange it is that we always think of the landscape as fixed when in fact it is constantly moving, constantly changing—dancing.

"Loss is about what's left," I say to Randy, not knowing what I mean.

CHAPTER SIX

Prairie Interrupted

It still reminds me of the benign sloping back of a brontosaurus, this prairie. Grey-green, in deepening or waxing shades depending on the time of year. It cleaves, leaving rounded backs of earth on either side. I guess you could say I feel I can pet them, stroke them as you would some creature, wild and exotic but tolerating your graces. I link this sensation to my familiarity with a place Pleistocene-like and yet young in human history.

Randy has disappeared into the demands of the hardware store. Weather, schedules keep me from the north Middle Alamosa. I'm back home, walking the farm.

What scuttles beside, below, and above me as I walk, that other commerce of the prairies? What teeming inheritors of the Pleistocene-cum-prairie persist in their unseen movements, their instinctive compasses? This prairie has been interrupted, after all, not free to simply remake itself but host to drought cycles, one-way plowing, conservation belts, terracing, the first barbed wire fences, overgrazing, as well as the digging of persistent badgers who can bring down a fence in no time. Perhaps it makes more sense to admit that such disturbances, human and natural, are all mixed up, each with their inherent order, for when you look at this groundswell of varied soils, for instance, it reads like slighted and dismembered documents—shapes of time that belie intervention.

We humans construct chronicles out of a wish to see time as sequential, somehow adding up. We photograph and map and name. Just in my lifetime, a new county road cut north from I-40, forming one border of our place. On the south side, where the Santa Fe Railroad tracks were removed, new fences reclaimed old track beds, and later satellite photographs provided the Agricultural Stabilization and Conservation Service offices with images of places they number "Farm 366" and "Farm 184." Perhaps more fitting a prairie so interrupted would be the scientific notion of time as a series of confluences or as intuitive roadways—more like the sense of our childhood meanderings than the fold-out maps of our educated years.

In a place—the apparently flat short-grass prairie—that begs a horizontal viewing as a reasonable perspective, I am reminded of a painting of beach and oceanfront life. The painter reframes the viewer's expectations, the perspective narrowed and from above, enforcing a vertical orientation instead. Beach and ocean meet vertical sky, canceling the usual languorous, horizontal, touristy view. Why not consider animal presence vertically as well? Yesterday's porcupine, which I had seen even earlier in the farm's last standing cottonwood tree, napping during the daytime, lolling on a thick limb, has a den somewhere underground. His nocturnal ramblings take him to weed and water sources, the bark of the large cottonwood completely stripped in his lifetime. He sleeps high in its naked remains. Winter takes him deep again, vertical, sleeping below as he slept above, having adjusted to the prairie as treeless reality. Perhaps the single old cottonwood was a dream come true, his mammal imagination letting him ride high for a few seasons until he had to avoid the cracked and dangerous limb of his own voraciousness—the death of his dream above ground.

I saw him again later, arthritic, exaggerated ambling from side to side, literally rocking down the road. Like so many animals at the farm, he crosshatches the area connecting feeding grounds to water sources. He has become horizontal again in his habits. And most recently I spotted him at the roadside, stripping kochia weed stalks as if they were the bark of a tree. He manages his vertical dreams on a different scale.

Bordering this same county road, the bar ditch had long been home, breeding and nesting ground, for a number of other species. Here—because of water run-off, a depth that holds moisture, even snow, and because of the benignness of the neighbor farmers who tend to the land inside the barbed wire fence, not out—varieties of the mixed prairie persist year after year. Such cover may be home to prairie box turtles repeating their amphibian habits, unaware of trucks that are larger and faster by the year. Given the low number of the annually laid eggs that survive natural predators, these turtles are particularly fortunate to be alive in the industrial world. When I find one crossing the gravel and caliche road I want to hurry her across. And cross she must! Such internal notion of place becomes a re-pacing of breeding and feeding grounds despite the raised roadbeds. More often than not I find a dead turtle, pale diamond-green shell smashed by one of those trucks, a flattened abstract design. Now here is, ironically, a "silent" nature that allows close examination of the shell, the head, the claws digging into death.

I've made a kind of fetish of noting the local animals fixed in some death throe. "Dead Animals of Oldham County," I say sardonically to myself as I stop to observe the remains of raccoons, coyote, mule deer, snakes, horned lizards—thinking of a poem or an essay on the topic. I photograph, redoubling stillness in a kind of curious hom-age to their momentary preservation before one more speeding car destroys them and the crows move in. Once I spotted some medium-sized animal killed on the access road by I-40 and pulled my old Jeep pickup off the road to take a look. It was a female badger, obviously with babies somewhere. Her teats were swollen and large, still full of milk. Her head was mostly unidentifiable, a bloody mass on the pavement, the remainder of the body fully mammalian, a mother's nocturnal search for food taking her into the motorists' "right of way." I have to ask myself: *When does a prairie become a pasture*, domesticated as someone's right of way? Days later she had all but disappeared into a dark spot, blushing the roadway.

Aerial vantage points would seem to show us a confluence of such interruptions, flattening time as they map contiguous space. The cultural geographer J. B. Jackson, editor of the early periodical *Land-scape*, initiated such revelations in his cultivation of the documentary art of aerial photography. I experienced this perspective once, flying in a private plane over the farm and grassland. I could see the conservation terraces built in the 1930s. I could also see they were built along a small series of leveled areas, like small plateaus, faintly different in color, suggesting perhaps a different soil type.

Later, on the ground, I discovered in a cache of old photographs made in the same area that the pasture I had seen from above had been part of an early Oldham County golf course. In the same manner that turn-of-the century settler Doc Lloyd printed brochures advertising Oldham Country as the "Garden" of the Panhandle, local boosters believed they could attract citizens to the town of Vega by building their own links. Sand greens were plotted on the up-slopes on either side of the prevalent draw on our place a few years before my dad bought the land. In an early 1930s photograph, local men with their scruffy clubs and bags chip golf balls out of a sand green. Conditions for play during the first Dust Bowl years must have made the sand green an ironic reminder of disappearing topsoil. I do wonder about that sand. Had it formed some soil basis in what is now another prairie mix, that varied soil and vegetation color so visible from my flight?

Ⅴ It has taken a half century for the grounded local farmers to envision putting down manure for "natural" fertilization, to bring back the tractored-out soil and overgrazed grasses of the Depression and the drought cycles. Cattle accomplish a measure of this, but they trample the grasses and crop and disrupt the seed cycles. Buffalo previously did indeed roam, leaving nourishing excrement behind but also because of their movement allowing for the natural replenishment of grasses. I have been watching an old buffalo wallow that is still visible in a corner of the south pasture, near the tilled land. Through the years I see its basin deepen and form the beginnings of a wash, which eventually will break down through wind and water erosion to form yet another route to the river, taking a part of the prairie with it.

Other more modern projects, like the dams along the central draw of this prairie, have done little to stop the persistence of water and topographic changes. The dam, built up to make a stock tank in the late 1920s, shortly after the prairie was first broken out for wheat farming in the Panhandle, lasted a while but collapsed in one of the high rises late in that decade. By the time I was old enough to go to the farm with my dad and grandfather, I thought of both sides of the broken dam as mountains (another dinosaur fantasy? another child's playground?), never in the practical ways they did. Later, during the thirties, the CCC guys built a dam of rocks hauled from the Canadian River back up stream. Another conservation effort, it has long been eroded by water forming around it a deeper channel of its will. The final attempt to dam the draw was my dad's. An amateur engineer, with his old Massey tractor he constructed a dirt dam above the CCC washout. That too proved folly in a country given to extremes. The infrequent but powerful high rises, racing water caused by heavy downpours, forced the soil from around the dam, leaving it ineffectual, a corner of the CCC rock dam downstream hanging in the air. My dad died of a heart attack one weekend while he was shoring up sections of the cracked dam and the eroding draw on the North Place. Days later I picked up a very small stone from the site to keep with me, as if I could hold those energies in my hand.

Just a mile from this pasture, two other landowners have tended their water in different ways, the latest with a fancy holding tank. This was the same rancher who decided to clear the mesquite and cholla cactus from the prairie and cross-fence it, ostensibly for a mother cow/calf operation. To "make" a prairie only promoted more loss of habitat; the lack of cover allowed for topsoil wash. Loss of original plant diversity changed the late summer arrival of the usual monarch butterfly population. That and consistent mowing of the bar ditches up and down this section compromised the natural nesting places for turtles, meadowlarks, and other creatures. From the bar ditches the larks once colored the sky with their mating calls, a rainbow of sound arching the country road. Now they are singular, largely silent. Up the road, the other neighbor never turns off his windmill. Water spills over the cattle tub, a waste, but its undulating run-off attracts seasonal avocets and the springtime's dancing sandhill cranes.

⩔ March 2005: I was in Kailua, Hawai'i, answering e-mails at a friend's house, when I read the one about the Panhandle prairie fires. Life by the ocean seems a long way from the mainland, but in particular from the Texas drought and the shock of fire. My longtime family friend, Ann Haliburton, then eighty-five, knowing that I was in Hawai'i on my spring break from the university, had e-mailed some of the details.

With mauka rains tinkling on the ti leaves, windows flush in undulating greens, and the salty smell of the ocean nearby, I tried to imagine fire. By sheer will I wanted to put out those distant fires. I feared visualizing my home prairie with sizzling ground noise, choking smoke, the unpredictable rage of crackling heat. The bunching of cattle, the need to cut fences, the rolling eyes of livestock replace the soft, rolling prairie I carry somewhere inside when away.

But I was in the tropics surrounded by water! I went online. I tried to read more. I held positive thoughts that did not have fire in them. Next day I read in the *Honolulu Advertiser*, on the last page of the national news section, a report on the still uncontained grass fire, already engulfing sixty thousand acres near Amarillo, Texas. It was a major national disaster story but mostly lost in the wake of Katrina and front-page war news.

My adult life had been one of such disconnections, often chosen interruptions. Shouldn't my "lifestyle" have prepared me for this? Yes, I spent my childhood through high school in Vega, Texas—as the town name indicates, the middle of the prairie. But I had moved several times since—college elsewhere, professional stints in New Mexico, Tennessee, Hawai'i, grants in New York State, the Northwest, Fulbrights in Eritrea, Portugal, Hungary, Poland, and Finland. Most of my university appointments were in urban places, in cities with a coastline, or a river or lake nearby. Like most kids reared in rural areas who leave home to make their lives elsewhere, I initially tried to replace the outlander's prairie life with something the outside world tells us is "better."

But I returned "home" regularly—summers, holidays, and for another job in the area when I inherited the Vega house of my great-aunt and -uncle and set about in my own modest "back to the land" movement. Meanwhile, the prairie remained inside, a grounding for my wanderings. Gradually, I came to see some continuities in supposedly unrelated places. One morning, when I first moved into the Chihuahuan Desert, on an escarpment ten miles northwest of El Paso, I awoke to see dense fog covering the farming valley of the Rio Grande below. In the distance were the Franklin Mountains, which run through the center of El Paso. The effect, similar to my ocean view in Lanikai near Kailua, Hawai'i, surprised me. I recalled what a friend of mine in Hawai'i related of a similar familiarity felt by visiting Hawaiians to Zuni Pueblo and the surrounding desert landscape. They felt at home in the dry relief of those mountains because they at once recognized them as ancient coral reefs, originally ocean. I felt perched on the backbone of metaphor—that transitory link of one place to another.

↓ Earth, air, fire, water. How basic the composition of our bodies within the world's body. I remembered the science book I had as a child. I still have it in my library. Fascinated by its survey of the great geologic periods, the flora and fauna of certain of the Earth's eras, the so-called cataclysms that changed them, I imagined myself stepping into the illustrated diorama of scientific chapter and verse. But the science of those 1950s books did not invite an understanding of continuities. Later research by folklorists studying dreams in the 1970s posited that survivals, remnants of the past, recur as elements in the accounts of dreams. Bedded in the subconscious are recognizable kernels—elements of longer narratives, recurring symbols, cultural remnants. These kernels reference portions of lost, older cultural stories and were identified as snippets that could potentially carry forward such elements, basic to myths in transition.

↓ By the time I got back to the Panhandle, to see things for myself, to walk the blackened prairie, to talk to devastated farmers and ranchers, wildlife managers, to look for the creatures who unseen by day had always left their tracks by night, I wondered additionally about wildfires of an earlier period, before the small farms and ranches, the human settlement. Prairie fires were regarded as natural, as inevitable. But that was before there was a built prairie.

One of the most shocking realities of the Panhandle fires, repeated over and over, was the fright of the cattle and horses. Early speculation was that muscles remember, that instinctively all animals, wild and domesticated, would try to escape as their ancestors had. They would run. Yes, some of the horses and cattle ran; yes, their owners cut fences, opened gates, tried to move them by horseback, truck, ATV, even by chasing on foot behind them. But there were numerous accounts of the ultimate confusion of these animals, how they froze fearfully in the face of fire, not knowing what to do, perhaps domesticated to a degree by our "care," by the habit of corral, lot, fenced pasture that bound them.

One of the accounts of the immediate aftermath of the fire brought this fact painfully home. A couple from Panhandle, Texas, sixty miles east of Amarillo, battled the unrelenting 60 mph wind and fire around their house and barns. They poured water, tossed shovels of dirt on orange, glowing pieces of wood that came within ten feet of their house. When the house was saved, the barn partially destroyed, the wife, Kathy, walked down to the corrals to look for the cats that had lived there and for various livestock, including the horses on the place. She came back in tears.

What she found was a young horse, still alive after the firestorms, in the corner of what remained of the barn. Apparently, the traumatized colt had stood bolt still as the fire nearly engulfed him and indeed burned his head and body. He still stood but with an awful shaking. Seeing his owner, he managed to stay up a few more moments, perhaps instinctively knowing he had to stand in order to live or waiting for his owner to rescue him. As she gently tried to approach him, he collapsed, lay on his side, eventually died.

Of course, the major concern—if one followed the front-page news in the *Amarillo Globe Times*, which ran daily that whole month, even after the fire's containment—was loss of human lives and property. Four people dead, 350,000 miles of fencing and farm structures damaged or destroyed, and about 960,000 acres scorched. The cost of replacing a mile of fence is five thousand dollars. Loss of livestock settled into about the five thousand head range rather than the originally estimated ten thousand. But the story of the colt—fixed in his suffering, his fright, his entrapment—stuck. Someone said that with so much loss—the atmosphere still filled by the gray of floating ashes—only something called spirit remained.

Ⱶ Back down in the Chihuahuan Desert, where I work at the local university, you live with aridity, an average humidity of 6 percent, annual rainfall six inches. No fire, but at least considerable heat, especially in the summers. Instead, a flood hits El Paso, dumping six inches of rain in two hours, following considerable moisture amounts in the previous days, eventually causing one hundred million dollars in damage and ravaging three hundred homes. At my condominium, my neighbor's silver-gray VW slips off into an arroyo drainage area, which rushes like Niagara. It was discovered later that the city, unlike the traditional *mayordomos* in the valley who tend the ditches, keeping them clear of debris, had not kept the area clean. Rocks and trash carried by the rushing flood undermined the stone and concrete sides, the parking lot caving into the drainage area. Off catapulted the Volks, nose down, filling so completely with the accumulating rocks and trash that only a work crew with picks and axes could get it out weeks after the storm.

But out in the surrounding desert, in fact even in town along the slopes of the Franklin Mountains and then up and down I-25 north all the way to Albuquerque, the desert bloomed. What should have been summer's heat-stressed plants looked spring-like. Local botanists, experts in desert flora, witnessed in amazement the blooming of species not seen in one hundred years. Along the highway thoroughfares caliche globe mallow reached an unprecedented height, creating a bright green, orange-tipped border in an area where there is usually more sand than plant life. Open space—that flesh-colored sand—was filled with green as far as the eye could see. For once this desert, a portion identified on maps as the Jornado de Muerto, now appeared to be a sea of grass.

⅄ My students and I stand in one of the arroyo washes, hands sheltering our eyes against the sun, some of us guarded by our black wrap-around sunglasses. Scott Cutler, a geologist and head of University of Texas at El Paso's Centennial Museum, holds up a photograph of the area from the Franklin Mountains to the Rio Grande basin showing the arroyo where we stand. "We are here," he says, pointing to the blue-green streaked section of the inkjet photo. I immediately feel slightly out of body, seeing where we are in the photograph yet simultaneously standing in the actual arroyo, looking up to where it runs to the Franklin peaks a couple of miles away. "It's hard to appreciate what is before us," he continues. "Like this rock for instance." (He bends to collect an oblong, white rock, seemingly nondescript, just palm size.) "Look at how it is smooth on all sides, obviously a rock washed from the flutes on the sides of the Franklin Mountains and down this arroyo." He had been talking to my students, creative writers, about the El Paso arroyo system, comprising some 250 arroyos, which came to everyone's attention during the recent flood. My idea is to get my students out of the classroom and physically into the environment, one I realized they largely had not experienced, even as El Paso natives. The subject of arroyos brings up the subject of plans for green space and conservation efforts in this city of half a million people.

But what Scott said next surprised everyone. Sure the mountain had loosed its elements, releasing stones that now covered this arroyo. They were everywhere; in fact, the arroyo itself was defined by thousands of fist-sized stones upon which we stood.

"It's hard for us humans to get our minds around the timeline of a rock," he said. "This one, for instance, is probably about thirty million years old, and it took some of that time for it to get down the mountain to where we stand. So we, with maybe a life expectancy of eighty years, are standing among stones whose movement took that long to get them to this place in the arroyo." I understood at that moment the nature of my odd feeling—what it means to be in a space between what something was and what it is becoming. And how this space, like the effect of time in Scott's photo, makes us aware of place—unfluted, transitional.

I thought of an earlier time in my life, when I had lived in another desert, the high desert near Albuquerque, New Mexico. Working as executive director for the New Mexico Humanities Council, a state branch of the National Endowment for the Humanities, I enjoyed particularly the guidance of three Native Americans, two Pueblo men and a Navajo, who were instrumental in our contribution to a funding project in Santa Fe at a local seed bank. The project undertook to provide nonhybridized native corn seeds from Tesuque Pueblo north of Santa Fe to parts of famine and drought-beset Ethiopia. The idea was that, unlike the hybridized seeds provided in some relief efforts, these were sustainable—the native seeds had a chance to come up year after year. The ambitious project entailed airdropping the color-coded seeds along with a tiny map-like illustration, which showed how to plant them. It seemed at once both a giant project and a small one. The idea of distributing seeds across the world, and in a country historically separated by formidable mountain ranges, river gorges, and desert, was daunting. The "humanities" part of the project had to do with the role of native seeds in cultural sustainability and how these could be shared with other desert dwellers on the other side of the globe.

Tesuque, surrounded by Santa Fe development, had until just recently ceased to have its yearly corn dance. The reason: the pueblo had stopped growing corn. Unlike other, more distant pueblos, Tesuque felt a labor drain from the pueblo to the non-reservation city. People left. Or they worked day jobs and only sporadically returned home. A particularly difficult result of this drain was that the ceremonies of planting and harvesting, essentially connected to the seasons, were lost, adversely affecting the transmittal of traditions to the young. To help, the Hopi loaned Tesuque some of their own reserve corn seeds. Some of the corn seeds given to Tesuque may have been "ancient" seeds, saved in storage jars for exceedingly dry seasons. With the planting of this corn at Tesuque came harvests and the return of ceremonial dances. From these corn harvests Tesuque donated seeds for relief in Ethiopia. I liked to think of the corn-filled packets sifting down from the aerial drops, distributing New World corn to the oldest cradle of humankind. If I had wondered through the years what it meant to return to landscape, now I asked what it meant for the landscape to return to us.

⅄ That next summer I went back home to Vega, which had been without rain for almost nine months, including the period of the fires in March. The town and Oldham County were recommending fire ditches not only around houses but also around entire pastures. I walked in a pasture about ten miles south of Armitage Farms, witnessing a specter. In the midst of the charred, blackened prairie were green and cholla cactus, still standing. How had the fire swept the ground around those cacti without taking them down? It could have been the height of the grass but also the moisture, the water content inside the cactus, that prevented them from catching fire.

Like everyone else, I opted for the fire lanes. Prairie left somehow unscathed was now systematically graded up into a lane about twenty

Cedar Breaks. *Author photo.*

feet across—the tractor blade scraping the natural turf down to the hardpan. The experience was visceral for me. I could feel the rip as in my own flesh. A kind of wound, this loss of habitat. I was reminded of how I feel when I pass the new developments, the "farmettes," going up along frontage roads west of Amarillo as the city grows at a sprawling rate. Native soil is scraped off, square acreage laid out, large, mostly two-story houses, lacking any environmental sense or historical style, quickly built. All finished out with new, thirsty Midwest sod. The new prairie ideal. The domestication of the short grass prairie. I felt that same tear as the soil, house to house for the fire lanes, was strafed aside.

West of these farmettes, a new wind energy field was going up, stretching into Oldham County. The company graded miles and miles of Canadian escarpment into the necessary large network of roads. All summer, up and down the connecting county road, trucks hauled water in a region known for its water shortage. I heard that east of Vega, near Pantex, the federal Department of Energy (DOE) plutonium dismantling facility, horny toads are fitted with small backpacks so they can be scientifically tracked to see if any potential pollution or habitat disruption at the site impacts their community. To the south was land earmarked in the DOE's records for the possible building of a high-level nuclear waste dump site.

ꜹ But for now we enjoy something very strange that happened this fall. Possibly it is an aspect of global warming, like the excesses of floods, fires, and droughts. A six-inch rain fell in two days on the blackened and blanched, burnt earth in the eastern Panhandle. A little more than that fell in the western Panhandle. It seems that almost overnight a consistent tall prairie grass—black grama—covers everything. This grass heads in a horizontal flag of darker seeds from the vertical parent stalk. From a distance, the undulation is a green topped with what looks like a faint but uniform magenta, thus a rich carpet close to the ground with softly moving lavender flags. The cattleman who leases our grassland held off for a month from putting his cattle back on the place because he didn't want to disturb the astounding beauty. Maybe part of his reluctance was the rarity of this much grass, this single variety dominating, this uniformity of beauty, which suggests that earlier epithet, "the sea of grass." There was a desire not to break it, interrupt it. While mowers whirled in town to tidy up yards gone ragged, out on the prairie people waited. Sometimes muscles—seeds, stones too—remember.

CHAPTER SEVEN

Dwelling

"Mom," my grandmother, is in the kitchen whipping up pancakes. She knows I love them, especially when she spoons the batter out in the shape of animals—horses, cows, birds. I wonder if she means to create them or if they have their own kettle will, oozing into something she can then name. The smell is mixed in my mind with maple syrup imagined ahead of time. Her arms, hefty and aging, flap according to how hard she stirs.

But so far nothing takes me away from the radio. I am sprawled on my stomach, tummy to worn carpet, wearing a two-piece summer shorts outfit. It's Saturday morning at my grandparents'. I usually sleep over to Sunday, when my parents pick me up for church. The old white radio, an early portable, sits in the middle of the living room, the center of my attention. I've turned off the lights, placed it by my tent, a card table with a blanket thrown over it. If Aunt Cleo were here I could tie her up to one of the table legs while I listen. Aunt Cleo sometimes plays my horse, getting on all fours and letting me ride her.

For years after my grandparents died this radio had a special place in my mother's attic, immune to occasional mass cleanings of accumulated "stuff," a prize from the yesteryears of my grandparents' house. I sometimes rooted my way back, past my mother's layers of Christmas ornaments, the stashed Kleenex and rolls of toilet paper, the stuffed toys (Elsa the cow, kittens with just the right expressions, my keepsakes), lamps that no longer worked but should nonetheless be saved in the opinion of my Depression-tempered mother, boxes of clothes she wasn't quite ready to give away. Who knows what else lurked in the attic? It was always an adventure, a draw, and had a special spicy smell of time gone by. *The radio no longer worked. Cord frayed, dials spun out. It had held such stories.*

I wiggle the dial. The reception is not good this morning, here thirty-five miles away from the broadcasting local station. I've got to hear this part. The opening thrills me. I ease my ear to the scratchy covering on front. "The Lone Ranger rides again."

It's Silver the horse I like, and of course Tonto. He's the mystery man, speaking in broken English, haltingly. I know he is smarter. I know without him the Lone Ranger wouldn't prevail. I listen to the episodes in hopes of some breakthrough of the kind when Rochester might best Jack Benny and take over the show. But history is a reluctant repentant. I already know this at some level from my schoolbooks bereft of Tontos or Rochesters, even as buffoons or second-class sidekicks.

Still I can't resist. The pull of the radio—knowing the basic plot and yet not knowing what comes next. Leaning into the story, I perk an ear.

"Come and get it," from the kitchen loops together with "This way, Kemo Sabe."

"But it's not over, Mom. Can I listen to the rest of the show?"

I hear a scraping of the pan. I know she is scooping out the fat browned pancakes into an aluminum pan, one of those bunged up, burned ones—nothing's new in my grandmother's house—and placing it, loaded with the stacks, in the warming oven.

⩔ Neither my brother nor I knew a thing about dugouts. Sure, we'd seen pictures and heard people talk about them, but we'd never been in one. I tried to imagine the slow dissolving of the mud-packed stones and wooden beams that formed their foundation. If nothing else the ravishing of the Dust Bowl would have filled them in. Like the sod house of the famous Dust Bowl photographs, they would have been only slightly better than the wall of wind that bent folks back and forth and permanently tilted trees, if any survived.

Not knowing about dugouts didn't keep my brother from building one. Out back of our house in Vega there was a hole. Who knew what caused it, but there it was, a cleavage that invited digging. With shovels and hoes, my brother and my cousin Jimmy got after it, more energy for this than for their daily chores. Below the topsoil layer, the Panhandle soil can be unforgiving. How they penetrated the caliche I have no idea, but in a day or two they had deepened and widened the caved-in place so that they could root around, shirts stripped off, like a couple of miners burrowing into a promising shaft.

Finally, after a few days, they disappeared in the hole it was so deep. They dug up under the lip of the hole so that the earth provided a kind of natural roof for their room. Little-sis-keep-out was written all over this boys-only experiment, but that didn't keep me from tagging along. Roy had a soft spot for his little sidekick even as the hideout, the dugout, mainly attracted his friends.

It all made perfect sense in a land without trees. Where else would one build a clubhouse? Besides it was cool and if you watched for spiders and snakes, the walls were welcoming to lean back against on a hot summer day.

We could have seen a real dugout had we known. My neighbor's father, Henry, born in 1904, was born south of town in a dugout. We could have at least learned some things about really living there, maybe even found some remnants south of town. Jess Giles, who built my Vega house in 1920, came west from Illinois as a young man, following the early wheat harvests when they first broke out the prairie. He, too, lived in a dugout. Like Roy's teenaged attempt, these early-day dwellings were dug directly into flat land, with the wooden door entry on top.

Winter came and the secrecy and exclusiveness of the dugout continued. The boys made bigger plans. They moved an old fuel tank, a cast-off from a combine, into the hole, filled it with a little gasoline, and lit a match, thinking it would burn inside and warm their clubhouse. Fumes and potential fire drove them out, and my dad, sniffing this disaster, made them fill in the hole in the dead of winter.

My uncle tells a story about his mother who had lived in a dugout. It's not a winter story but suggests what daily life must have been like. He visited his aging mother, who suffered dementia, and to pass time, he urged her to talk about her early married life on the prairie, in the dugout. What was it like? With some coaxing and filling in of details, he learned that she had meticulously collected glass containers, like old jelly jars, to use for drinking and had labored to keep such containers clean. Later, when she was near death and unable to talk anymore, she on occasion raised her hands and moved them in a circle, as if she were still washing and drying the glasses.

⌄ Ysabel must have built his dugout in the late 1870s. A surviving photo shows the structure banked into a slope of Alamosa Creek (later known as the Middle Alamosa), which rises maybe twenty feet above the then narrow and relatively deep creek. Similar to the architecture of houses in Anton Chico, New Mexico, where Ysabel was born, the dugout is made of stacked local stone and mud mortar, combined with adobe bricks for stability and support. Like the Stone Age people before him, Ysabel used what the land provided. Vigas—large cottonwood logs that helped support a grass and mud flat roof—show on the lateral sides of the structure. But most impressive are the two front buttresses, semicircular stacked rocks that buffer each side of the front door and provide a mooring against the incline of the cliff. Unlike the plains dugouts with necessarily horizontal openings following the flatland's contour, Ysabel's place made use of the slope leading to the river—-more a half-dugout, with a portion dug into the cliffside itself. Ysabel seems to have brought part of Anton Chico with him. The front of the Catholic church there—still celebrating mass today—is a Spanish colonial adaptation with twin fronting buttresses, a possible inspiration for Ysabel's front design.

No doubt Ysabel brought more. Though plain to the point of austerity, the one-room dwelling likely would have a wooden bed with leather or wooden slats, a mattress stuffed with straw or wool, a colorful Saltillo woven blanket for a bedcover, and probably a woven rug for the dirt-packed floor. A hand-hewn table and chair or maybe a small cupboard would complete the room. Tin-framed images of the saints may have hung on one of the walls. A trunk provided storage for clothes and other things, keeping mice and packrats at bay.

Later Ysabel would build a house nearby and begin his family there. It's this collapsing adobe that Randy and I now hike toward. But I hold the image of the dugout in my mind. The Middle Alamosa ran deep back then, proved by the water-sculpted, mostly dry landscape I'd been traveling these past four summers. And in the photograph, the bow-legged man with the Stetson hat in front of the dugout reminded me of how my dad's story hastened to connect with Ysabel's.

I'd been to Ysabel's Camp several times through the years, but always came by a ranch road that approaches it from the east. One time Sheriff David Medlin, decked out in his official gear swathed in a hefty gun holster, jeans, vest, the ever-present cowboy hat, and his distinctive handlebar moustache, who shared my love of the breaks country, offered to drive me around. He essentially circled what would become my hiking route, approaching the Middle Alamosa from the east, stopping often for views of its enormous and spellbinding valley, noting grinding holes, and telling stories of Billy the Kid's hideout located in a canyon off the Middle Alamosa Creek valley. We stopped off at Ysabel's at the far north end of our trip, then looped around past Little Arrowhead and back toward Vega.

Today's route, following the creek bed and on foot, dramatizes the insistent energy of the landscape's history, its circuitous fruition, its persistent will, and now its impending culmination in the Canadian. This summer of 2007 is a wet one. The creek runs red from rain-washed clays and silt, wide and shallow—more like a washed roadway than a creek. Against the radiant blue sky speckled with small white clouds, its colors remind me why Georgia O'Keeffe first fell in love with the llano and its canyon lands. Her first stop in the Southwest had been Canyon, Texas, where she taught art at the fledgling West Texas Normal School and walked weekends all the way to Palo Duro Canyon to paint.

I photograph—a distant second to her iridescent imagination—and I walk.

The previous summer, Randy and I located a sizeable bog and pastured valley near the confluence of the Canadian and its tributary. Here Ysabel's choice of settlement was borne out by historic sheep pens, walls constructed like Ysabel's dugout of stone slabs. We'd been told a wagon depot or a stage stop had been near here and that this valley had been a popular buffalo grazing ground. Called "the Jog" on ranch maps to designate the location and shape of this pasture, the deep grass was protected by large cottonwoods on the east, indicating either springs or a very low-lying area near the river. Close to Boys' Ranch, formerly historic Old Tascosa, the second town established in the Panhandle, in 1880, the area attracted people from the Archaic period on with its reliable water, wildlife, forage, and wood.

Up above the bog on a slight slope, we discovered these layers of settlement: a porcelain doorknob, a nail from a mule's iron shoe, Ali-

Near confluence of Middle Alamosa Creek and Canadian River. *Author photo.*

bates worked flint, Tecovas points, and the telltale sheep pens built by the pastores, the Hispanic and Mexican sheepmen who were the first non-Native men to settle in the area.

"Frenchy's doorknob," Randy joked, referring to the well-worn story of Frenchy's odyssey from nun in New Orleans to dancehall girl in Tascosa.

"But it's only to Mickey's room," I responded—referring to Mickey, the livery stable owner whom Frenchy fell for, and we guess reformed for. They married. The two are subject of a long-standing romantic story of Tascosa, one that balances its reputation of as a wild-West town full of drunken cowboys whose shoot-outs made the town famous for its Boot Hill Cemetery.

Frenchy pledged to stick by her Mick forever and proved it by being the last citizen of the cowtown, still living alone in a crumbling adobe years after Mickey's death. I loved to hear her story when I was a girl, imagining her boldness in purportedly running away from the Louisiana nunnery, then getting herself to Tascosa and finding the man of her dreams. The story was fueled in my imagination by a photograph of Frenchy. A family friend, Roy Turner, who owned a ranch near Tascosa, had a photo album in which both Mickey and

Frenchy were prominently displayed. Frenchy babysat Roy when he was a child. Frenchy, bedecked in sumptuous ruffles and trailing skirt, leans lightly on a gate fronting a lush country setting—part of the studio photographer's prop and a far cry from Tascosa's notoriously muddy—or dusty—streets. Mickey, in a companion photograph, looks dashing with a small moustache and riding attire. Frenchy is beautiful, with a shapely body and a Clara Bow face. Here is the local version of Matt Dillon (almost) and Miss Kitty.

Mother would have remembered all this and more. Mother, Dorothy Mae Mesa. She did remind me once that Roy Turner had seen to Frenchy in her old age and had himself told a sad story of her loneliness. Long after Tascosa had disappeared, after the county seat moved to Vega and the much-needed railroad line passed through Amarillo, Frenchy lived alone, mostly with her memories. She kept a trunk with her wedding dress in it. Travelers from off the state highway, usually curious about Boot Hill and the gun battles in Tascosa, would discover her adobe and quiz her about the old times. Roy said he found her one day, fingering the wedding dress, recounting her fear of these intruders upon her still world. Frenchy was deaf.

The rough land may seem more a man's story, the cowboy and ranch history so prominent, but it was Mother who collected historic photographs, Mother who took me to visit Mr. Turner, and another time John McCarthy, who had written a book about Tascosa, Mother who knew Dulce Sullivan, Roy's sister-in-law, who wrote the definitive book on the LS Ranch, which Ysabel worked for. How I missed Mother's vice-like little hand asking for me to stay, stay, that giggle, the tender but strong and curious woman, the curly hair persistent into death. At the Jog, I reached into the detritus to find something defined by her memory—something to make up for my mere suppositions.

On the evening of her funeral I came back to be by myself, by the graveside again. I'd had to plan the funeral from afar. I had been in El Paso when she died. All those years of trying to be there for her, only to receive Donna Walton's message "she passed to the other side" one day after I returned to work in El Paso, thinking she was going to be "okay" a little longer. Again, as with my dad's premature and sudden death, there was no closure. I wanted to be by her side when she died.

I ordered a blanket of red roses to cover her casket. They covered the grave now. Such startling beauty in a prairie cemetery where the only trees to survive are arborvitae and a few elms. My dad had raised roses in his garden at their house. He relished picking a particularly full Peace rose for her, pink-tipped, a blush of bursting health. Roses were her favorite flower.

I wandered from the graveside. I should be relieved. Mother had suffered. I had suffered with her. But the caring during decline— what was it, twenty years now?—doesn't know where to go. Freedom doesn't ease the sweet pain of love. I hoped the Panhandle winds would take it—the ache of memory initially sharpening loss—but mainly I wandered.

That's when I came upon Ysabel's grave. I knew he had moved his family from out on the ranch to Vega and vaguely knew he was buried here, but I never thought of actually visiting the grave. And here it was, in a row of Gurules—wife, and apparently daughters. According to the cemetery records, born 1847, died 1936. Mother would have known him for only four years. She and Daddy married in 1932. But she would have known about him longer than that. He was born one hundred years before me. He died the year before my brother, Roy, was born.

I discovered from the woman who manages the cemetery for the county that some of the Gurule family used to come from New Mexico or wherever they moved (no one seemed to know) to decorate the graves. But no one had been here in a long time. I resolved to bring flowers—maybe roses—the next Memorial Day.

⩔ Randy let me out about a mile beyond our mothers' mesas for the final walk in. He was smoking a cigarette at the East Prong Windmill and assuring me he would head toward Ysabel's to meet me later. Randy has some health problems, holdovers from heat stroke, blood sugar issues. The past summer he had given me a scare.

After several tries, we'd found Billy the Kid's hideout, supposedly a place he hid stolen horses during the brief time he was in Tascosa. We'd laughed about it many times during our search, mainly because Randy had to consult several times with Roy, the ranch manager, about its location. After three aborted trips based on notes on a yellow pad, Roy put yellow ribbons on the juniper trees to show the way through the dense and roadless Cedar Breaks to a canyon's edge. There the trail seemed to play out. Randy and I climbed down the cliff; he went one way and I, the other. By sheer serendipity I found another tree with the telltale ribbon and after looking around a bit, realized it designated yet another little canyon, which I scrambled into. There I found the remains of a rock room that turned out to be Billy's hideout. I could see from the layout, again near a dried-up feeder creek, that he could have hidden horses. The broad Middle Alamosa Valley lay beyond—again, that highway. After trekking back, calling and calling, I linked up with Randy. I showed him the site, but on the boulders below he collapsed. Heat exhaustion? Low blood sugar? It was near sundown by that point, and my mind raced with possibilities . . . how the hell I would get him out of there? Finally, after many tries—Randy limping along, me, lamely lending a shoulder—we made our way to the pickup.

This time I was happy for him to enjoy his smoke; I felt like a young mare given her head and bolted on.

We'd been told of a site far west along the Canadian, at Salinas, another pastores site, where you could reach your hand deep into the salt pits and pull up flint shards. Digging just a few inches into the soil earlier at the Jog, we had brought up remnants, layers of the past. I remembered Ysabel had once helped run a freight line and later a stagecoach line that passed from Tascosa along the Canadian to Salinas and then to Las Vegas, New Mexico. Was this the connection between the Jog and Salinas? The stops were the pastores settlements, the route originating in their first forays into the Canadian River Valley.

⋁ They came from Anton Chico, Mora County, and Las Vegas, New Mexico. The lush valley vegetation and ample spring waters had no doubt made the area known before this *entrada*. A sheepman named Baca is said to have run thirty thousand sheep in what is now the Oklahoma Panhandle as early as 1863. Most authorities cite a firm date for the attempt at permanent settlement as shortly after the Red River Wars, in which the Comanche were defeated and removed to the reservation.

They followed the well-worn trails of the earlier Comancheros, and before them, the Indians and the Spanish. The Major Stephen Harriman Long expedition records noted that the Indians of the region seemed to have interacted with the Spanish from a very early date. In 1805, a Caddo Indian told John Sibley that he had visited and traded in Santa Fe forty years before. According to historian J. Evetts Haley, this trade was well established by the mid-eighteenth century.

As the trade continued to grow, three major trading areas and related trails were used in the Panhandle. When Colonel Charles Goodnight came to the Panhandle from Colorado in 1876, the date of the earliest pastores immigration, he observed that there were three Comanchero trails almost "as plain as the wagon roads of today." Of the three major trails, the upper trail left Las Vegas, New Mexico, and went northeast to the Canadian River, following the Canadian down to east of Tucumcari Mountain, and then forked at the Texas line. The left-hand fork led down the Canadian along the Fort Smith road to a trading ground at Las Tecovas Springs near Amarillo. Atascosa, or "boggy springs," was a major trading site on the way to Tecovas. Before the pastores and Comancheros, the *cibolleros*, or Spanish buffalo hunters, had used these trails.

We can only speculate the range of trade. According to Josiah Gregg, from about 1830 to 1840 the trade of the Comancheros was in "a few trinkets and trumperies of all kinds, and perhaps bread and another of pinole" to barter for horses and mules. In later years, the traders enlarged their stock to include ammunition, lead, musket pistols, knives, calico, wines, whiskey, and breads of all kinds. Yes, breads! A son of a prominent Anton Chico trader, Apodaca Anaya, reported that the *panocha*, "a bread that the Indians liked like the devil," was made by grinding sprouted wheat upon the metate, sweetening it with masa, and baking it in pones, much like the corn pones of today. According to Gregg the first traders, walking with packed mules or, if wealthier, driving carretas full of goods, simply relied on chance meetings with the Indians. As trade grew, places like Atascosa and Paint Rock became sites specifically designated for the trade, particularly in stolen cattle and horses.

In November 1876, Casimero Romero of Mora County, New Mexico, led a large party to Atascosa Creek, where Tascosa would later be founded. A former Comanchero trader, Romero was familiar with the spring sites along the Canadian, and knew the Atascosa as one of the most famous meeting places of the Mexican traders and Comanche and Kiowa Indians. A man of some wealth, Romero traveled with his family in a fine enclosed carriage, with twelve or more freight wagons following, each drawn by four yoke of oxen. He led possibly a dozen employees and three friends, with their families, who would also seek out spring sites for their home building. The wagons carried household goods, lumber, ranch equipment, and miscellaneous supplies to help weather the coming winter. Trailing behind were three thousand head of sheep and another fifteen hundred belonging to Agapito Sandoval, as well as several horses and enough cattle to provide beef and milk for the settlers for a year.

The group initially camped by Rica Creek, at a bend in the Canadian River where they would be sheltered by the towering cottonwoods that still mark the site today. They literally circled their wagons, filling in the intermediate spaces with tumbleweeds and brush, and stayed for almost a year until plazas could be built. After the winter, the men set about to choose building sites for their plazas—adobe houses, acequias, or waterways, to convey the spring water for personal and livestock use, and stone pens for protecting their prime economy, sheep. With the open grazing available, the pastores circulated the sheep throughout these Canadian valleys, seeking the good grass between Texas and the Pecos River area they came from. Boquilla Plaza, Salinas Plaza, Chavez Plaza were but a few of these settlements, and their populations ranged from twenty-five people at Salinas to almost one hundred at Chavez.

Ysabel came with his cousin and his family, sometime after the arrival of Romero. Whenever this was—1877 or so—his cousin was killed in an Indian attack, a reminder that there were still a few holdouts from the army. Some say Comanche, some, Pawnee. "If the attackers were Pawnee," I think, "how ironic if the gene pool had returned." I am thinking of the speculation among archaeologists that the last of the Antelope Creek Phase people may have joined the Pawnee. Could they return several generations later as marauders rather than agriculturalists? In any case, the cousin's family decided to return to Anton Chico, and only Ysabel and his brother, Hondo, stayed.

⋎ I am close now. The Middle Alamosa swells with the joining of the West Alamosa and I try to imagine what Ysabel would have seen the first time he visited this canyon. From the photograph of him by his dugout, the Middle Alamosa must have run deep and strong. Because of the massive buffalo slaughters the large herds would have all but disappeared, but he would have known the buffalo plains where small herds survived. Later, part of the income of freighters was earned by collecting the buffalo bones that bleached the plains between Tascosa and Dodge City for resale to be turned into fertilizer. Deer, antelope, and turkey abounded, as did the signature grapes and plums of the Canadian and its tributaries. Duck, prairie chickens, blue and bobwhite quail were plentiful. Beaver and beaver dams appeared along the Canadian, which, as a deep, narrow channel, provided drinkable water. As late as 1928—a couple of years after my dad's family moved to Vega—another photo taken of Wildorado school children shows two enormous black bears strung up behind them; bear, cougar, and lobos were still about then.

José Ynocencio Romero, the son of Casimero Romero, provided an extended account of the territory when the first pastores came in an interview given to Ernest R. Archambeau in 1946 for *The Panhandle Plains Historical Review*. Like Ysabel, he'd witnessed the great buffalo herds and their passing, the building of Tascosa and its demise, and he had worked the freight lines from Tascosa to Dodge City, Kansas—all of which Ysabel would have seen. "The buffalo watered by the thousands at the river and creeks around us and at the spring from which we got our irrigation water," he commented in the interview. "In winter they came down into the breaks for protection from the weather, and we could see them almost any time grazing the high grass in the river bottoms." Buffalo meat and jerky were the initial staples of the early pastores, until "the Eighties when we had to go up on the head of the Cheyenne and Tascosa Creeks when we wanted to kill a buffalo."

Along with the disappearance of the buffalo and the Indians, Romero commented on the changes of the river valley and river, which Ysabel would have witnessed as well. In the days before cattle ranching, the river was narrow and deep and clear, probably no more than twenty feet wide. Romero noted, "It was deep and there was always cold, clear water running between high, steep banks which were lined with a thick growth of bushes. Plums grew in abundance along the banks." When the Romero family first came, the men had to dig the banks down so that they could ford the river. Later, the coming of the cattle changed it. "They grazed down the tall grass in the river bottoms and destroyed the bushes along the banks. Whatever the reason, I know that after the cattle came the river changed from a narrow, deep river to a broad sandy waste with little water in it except to flood. Before the river filled up with sand, it was well stocked with fish, and the restaurants in Tascosa regularly served fish they caught with a seine in the river."

Romero recalled that when they first came to the Canadian country, the trail they followed on the south side of the Canadian was not well marked and they often had to skirt the heads of arroyos and creeks by taking long detours onto the plains. Few other people lived along the Canadian River, and he saw no evidence of previous settlers. At that time there was one man who lived on the river near Logan, New Mexico; the only other man they knew of in the territory lived in Mobeetie in the eastern Panhandle.

The Romero house was built of the same materials as Ysabel's adobe, but it was an impressive affair. The men made the adobe brick, dug an irrigation ditch from the springs for a large truck patch, and planted cottonwood seedlings, which grew to shade the house. The truck gardens included onions, cabbage, sweet corn, melons, peppers, and other vegetables. The walls and partitions were eighteen inches thick, the roof enhanced by lumber brought from New Mexico sawmills, then layered with about two inches of mud followed by eighteen inches of dirt on top. The house was over fifty feet long and about forty feet wide, with floors of packed earth. Corrals were built on the north side of the house. Sod and stone fences completed the corral. The house, according to Romero, was very comfortable, with wood-burning fireplaces in each room. Cooking was done on a cast iron cookstove in the kitchen and also in an outdoor adobe oven. In the plaza settlement everyone did washing over fires outside and often cooked over open fireplaces in the houses. Some houses were furnished with water via holes dug near the springs where water would gather and clear. The men cropped alfalfa and oats and cut prairie hay from the supple meadows. Other supplies were bought from Las Vegas and Dodge City and hauled over those trade routes. Romero speculates that by 1882, right around the time Tascosa was founded, approximately one hundred Mexican and Spanish people lived in the vicinity of Tascosa.

One of the best accounts of wildlife and daily life during Ysabel's early years along the Canadian comes from the *Tascosa Pioneer*, the weekly newspaper owned and operated by C. F. Rudolph from 1886 to 1891. In the *Pioneer*, in almost diary fashion, Rudolph chronicled the life of a frontier town. In a Saturday, June 26, 1886, article he wrote: "A hunting expedition that had been out and down through the Panhandle of Texas recently and returned to Garden City, Kansas report that they had seen . . . about three thousand buffalo in all, in small scattered bunches." "Eighty-six wild horses had been captured on the plains up to last week. . . . 'Mustanging' in the Panhandle shows up some profits." Rudolph described an ice business garnered from the frozen Canadian in winter that allowed the community to have an occasional fish-fry out of season. He waged war on the local bachelors, advocating marriage so as to expand the community. Most of all, he championed the possibility of a railroad in the near future that would guarantee Tascosa expansion and consistent commerce possibilities.

Rudolph also wrote about the closing of the plains, something that would affect the pastores in general and Ysabel specifically. "The Capitol Freehold and Investment Company, Limited—called the XIT for short—has under construction a very considerable amount of new fencing. So has the Lee-Scott company. Both ranches are receiving immense supplies of wire, and giving employment to a good many hands, building fence and freighting" (June 26, 1886). As many as ninety thousand head of cattle were still estimated to go up the Dodge City trail that June, but the Panhandle was rapidly being converted to privately owned ranch land. As cattlemen began buying up the range, they used various tactics to flush out the sheepmen. Random events, like the murder of a California family transporting a load of gold by a Hispanic bandit, set off a rampage of revenge that drove a number of the pastores out in fear for their safety. Various laws enacted by the Texas legislature defined the pastores as "drifters" and thus subject to dismissal from the land and to certain taxes on their herds. If they didn't leave there were instances of burning their houses and property. But the stereotypical rancher-versus-sheepman Hollywood gambit did not exactly play out since the sheepmen mostly respected the legal closing of the open range. After only ten years, and with pressures from the ranchers and Texas state laws preventing open grazing by the sheepmen, the pastores returned to New Mexico.

Ⅴ Ysabel stayed again, this time as a hand on one of the ranches. He worked as a cowboy for the remainder of his life for the LS Ranch, later Mansfield's. Ysabel's Camp—the dugout site, the adobe house—was now a cow camp, first manned by Ysabel but later, when he moved with his family to Vega, by various section cowboys. Jack Cauble, that wiry five-foot guy who no horse could shake, spent a considerable time in the camp, scratching the calendar days on the kitchen door to keep count. Hotdog McKendrie weathered a blizzard there in 1946, leaving his family in town and staying at the cow camp, where he fed cattle all winter by horse-drawn wagon.

Both my dad and Ysabel were of the horse-and-wagon generation, despite the difference in their ages. Dad told stories of plowing with a mule in Arkansas, and his childhood stories were full of pranks that reminded me of my brother's own goofy shenanigans. One of his mule stories had to do with "Red," a stout and stubborn mule who predictably resisted the plow but would run toward the barn when the day's work was done. One time Dad, thinking he would take a break too, tried to ride Red home. He was bucked off immediately and spent the rest of the time coming in from plowing trying to catch up to Red and figuring out how to save face. As a schoolboy he made going to his rural Arkansas school a game by stretching his body through the wagon spokes so he could turn over with the wheel on the way, like it was a carnival ride. He learned to ride a horse at an early age and to be the jack-of-all-trades a man of that generation needed to be—especially out in the country.

My grandfather tried the navy, the forest service, sharecropping, orchard management, and farming, and he worked as a printer. His son, perhaps no wonder, had two jobs all his adult life. Granddad lived in Arkansas, Oklahoma, Washington, New York, and in South Texas and the Panhandle of Texas by the time he was in his early forties. His son, declining administrative job offers in Dallas banks, stayed in a small town, wearing his starched white shirt to the bank until four o'clock, then changing into the blue work shirt and heading to the farm. He managed a small herd of cattle and farmed the two sections by himself.

I see my dad in his pickup, grin on his face, that grin lined with fine dirt that accumulates when he is plowing. He comes home sweaty, the blue shirt wet and colored with soil, his pants caked, his boots scuffed. He has horses. We round up the cattle and brand them. He watches hopefully over the tender wheat and maize plants. We "check" the cattle. Ride the fences. Walk into the middle of the planted fields to check the crops. Like Ysabel, my dad adapted to what presented itself. And like Ysabel, he honored old hats and sat a horse well. He stayed put.

⍒ Rain.

I think of what Rudolph wrote about the potential danger of Panhandle storms: "Many a pig and sheep turned its toes to the daisies"—his reference to a hailstorm in a country with little cover. Randy catches up with me early—I've slipped in between two high mud pinnacles that break the wind-driven rain—but I'm already soaked from the cloudburst and slogging through the wet sand. We pack it in for the day. On the way home, we take a couple of wrong turns. The ranch roads seem to change daily on Mansfield's: more oil drilling, more oil roads. The old route is crossed and crisscrossed. In the distance we see the new economy of the prairies: miles of wind turbines to the east toward Wildorado. They are rumored to be making their way west, crossing, somewhere, the Middle Alamosa. I consider this news bad luck, a violation.

Back home I dust off Dulce Sullivan's book on the LS, the Lee and Scott ranch that Ysabel first worked for, and find a couple of photos of ranch cowboys where Ysabel is identified. I drag out the magnifying glass, trying to see more. Here he is with that telltale Stetson hat the cowboys said he wore so many years it flopped down over his eyes. What was it that made a person like Ysabel stay? In a country with a basic economy of grass, whose commerce depends on trade and exchange, all of which creates a network of movement through time, the Canadian breaks attracted traders, not settlers. As historian

Elliott West points out in *The Future of the Southern Plains*, the plains resources were often overlooked; or when seized, were sent outward. The "energy" of the plains, primarily its grasses, was commercialized through the bison-centered cultures—Archaic man, the cibolleros, Comanches—whose harvesting of the plains creatures enabled a sophisticated network of trade in which every aspect of the bison was used. Alibates flint, too, was an industry, the hard and beautiful dolomite mined and traded from the time of Clovis man until 1870, when it was last mined before the removal of the Comanche and Kiowa. Movement of goods and people—even slavery, which was a part of historic Panhandle economy—marked the region, not settlement.

For many in the generation of my parents, the Dust Bowl also reinforced the early chroniclers' declaration of the plains as the Great American Desert. We know about those who left and why, but what about those who stayed? Maybe a man like Ysabel, who had lived within dirt walls like a prairie dog but sat astride a horse commanding a prairie view, knew a thing or two about dwelling.

⅄ The radio went the way of the Elvis Presley record "You Ain't Nothing but a Hound Dog," the 1940s Brownie camera, and my grandmother's gardening bonnet. I didn't mean for any of them to sell in the estate sale, but I was so busy hiding my grief, pretending to move forward, that they slipped right out the door. Frankly, I think the estate sale manager stole the Sun label record. He'd arranged and priced everything and remarked at the time that this was a "collectible." Maybe everything in my mother's house was that. Evelyn Taylor, one of her lifelong friends, who talked so fast and incessantly that her husband said until he got a hearing aid he thought Evelyn was chewing gum, said to me: "Shelley, why are you selling this house? You could turn it into a bed and breakfast, with each room a period piece." Well said, Evelyn. So why don't *you* do it? Of course I wasn't that rude.

Just mad. Mad and mostly scared. I didn't feel up to making the necessary decisions by myself.

The only daughter, this all falls to the only daughter.

Moving my mother to assisted living translated into a rocky last scene. Everything had sold. The house was bare, the wall-to-wall shag carpet seemed to stand up and take notice. My mother sat in her recliner, the only remaining piece of furniture in the living room. She didn't move. She was diminutive, my mother, a shoe salesman's size 4 dream, and when I leaned over her I felt like an ogre.

"Mother, if you absolutely don't want to go . . ."

Just a week before I had circled a mountain of Tupperware stacked in the middle of the living room, twirling my newly rediscovered high school baton through my fingers, with the cat-eyed, rhinestone-studded glasses of junior high snugly on my nose—circling like the stereotypic Indian getting ready for a sacrifice of the non-natives—when Ann, another of mother's friends, walked in.

"Are you having a nervous breakdown?" She was serious and even called me later to see if I was okay.

Sure, I'm okay. No, I am not. Where is my brother in all this? But even the nurses at the hospital where mother had her CAT scan reminded me: *It always falls to the daughter.* But why? This is a sixties gal you are talking to—Second Wave and all that. A feminist scholar. A PhD whose career demanded publications, conferences, and as I defined myself as the university's utility outfielder, an endless number of new courses to prepare.

Last time I had to argue with one of Mother's doctors—trying to get him to sign for Home Health Care because she lived alone and kept falling—I tried that gambit. He had been dismissive of both my mother and me.

"You may be a medical doctor," I said stiffening my back, moving close to his six-foot-five frame, shifting my weight as if readying for a Wild West shootout. "But I am a doctor too."

Really?

Why was my brother's career, life, family more important than mine? Besides, Roy was an EMT, a volunteer fireman, he loved being around emergencies, hospitals. Give him five minutes in such a place and he was on first-name basis with the staff and, more importantly, the doctors.

I didn't expect Roy to do it all. I had been his little sis sidekick. All I wanted was a partner.

It comes to the daughter. Roy was downstate, in Katy, Texas, a suburb of Houston. He had lots of responsibilities besides his job, I understood, and here was a long ways away. But he hadn't been to see Mother since the time my Weimaraner, Elsa, ran off at the farm, chasing some phantom quail down a draw. Roy and I stayed until dusk, calling, calling. And next morning he got up before dawn, went back out there, and found Elsa sitting by a tractor at the spot where she had taken off. He brought her safely home.

This was the big brother I knew: a protector, an advocate, a loving teaser, a guy who always let his little sister tag along.

But Roy had left Vega, left the farm, never to return. He attended college for a while, dropped out. He joined the navy, later worked in a bank, then for Northern Natural Gas, manning the enormous computer screens that controlled the flow of natural gas to six states. For a while he and Sue and the boys came up in the summers. My dad bought horses for the boys, their own saddles; we took photographs of the men crammed into the tractor cab, all smiles. I had always hoped he and I would run the farm together one day. But he was another one who by necessity left the Panhandle, left the plains.

I couldn't talk to Roy, I mean seriously, about Mother's condition, about the farm, finances. I never really thought of him as the strong, silent—and therefore, noncommunicative type. He was a joker, a cut-up. "*Your* mother," he would say to begin and end our "conversations."

I never expected to end up with the farm, run it alone. I always thought we would do it together after both parents were gone. Pardners, partners.

Here I thought I had disposed of Dale Evans's horse forever and was riding Roy Rogers's Trigger. By age five I had shed the Dale Evans Naugahyde skirt for red shorts but kept the six-guns slung low on my hips. I can still smell the exploded caps, sharp in the nose, feel the red, gabardine weskit, the tip of the Stetson hat slung back from my head. As a scholar I published a piece called "Rawhide Heroines." Hadn't we revised the Old West? Me, Tonto; you, Kemo Sabe.

Two days before my dad died of a massive heart attack in his shower in Vega, he was moving some large rocks into an eroded area in the North Draw—right about where you have the best view of the distant canyons to the north. He was stacking the large stones into the banks. It was a mere stopgap at best. This was a man whose father had gathered his wife and children to flee one of the worst floods in Arkansas delta history, driving the cattle to higher ground, sending his daughter on her horse to warn the sharecroppers, returning in a row boat later to rescue the family cat perched in the attic window as the river rose to the second story. A river, even this intermittent creek bed, will have its way.

He'd come back to town thinking he had a case of heat exhaustion.

I have a photo of my dad and my brother at Cloudcroft, New Mexico—tall, fit man, small blond Jackie Coogan-looking boy. There's a trace of seriousness, maybe awkwardness. The grown man, his arms firmly wrapped around the boy's shoulders; the boy seeming to hold up under the pressure.

As for my brother, it was his cancer that brought us closer together again. I later recalled his gray color and eyes with dark circles under them at my mother's funeral, but none of us knew he might be sick then, not even him. The cancer was discovered more than a year later when he complained of back pain. I phoned him almost daily; we mostly revisited our childhood days. I could tell the calls helped. I struggled to sound upbeat, nonchalant. My heart was breaking for him. No matter what, I always deeply loved my brother.

"Are you still throwing around that twirling baton?"

"What do you mean?"

"You know, like the time you threw it at Jimmy and me and broke out Mother's louvered windows in the living room."

"Ho! You and Jimmy teased me to death all the time. I had to throw that to get you guys away from me. Or was it that I was just a bad twirler?"

"Yeah, you were a bad twirler all right, aiming at Jimmy and me and hitting the windows instead!"

Getting Roy to muster even the faintest laugh was an achievement. He was fixated on "the numbers"—the weekly readings of his blood count indicating how severe the cancer was. He believed he could get it into remission.

"Are you still smoking?"

"You know I never smoked in my life."

"Now wait a minute. Remember that faded old pink bunny rabbit, that stuffed toy with the zipper in back? The one you took to slumber parties when you were a kid?"

"Hmmm."

"And how you hid those awful menthol cigarettes in that zipped pouch—instead of your pajamas?"

"Hmmm. Yeah, well, what do you expect of a fourth grader? We went through that phase where we thought we could be like the adults if only we could smoke. I went to the drug store asking Joe for Salem menthols for my daddy. Joe would give me a look; Daddy smoked Marlboros."

"Yeah, but you did it in my room, remember? I was the first to find you back there with the door closed as if nobody could smell those horrible menthol ciggies."

"Hmm, yeah, and you said, 'You better stop that or Mother will find you and give you a whipping.'"

"And I said, 'Mother never gives me a whipping.'"

"And you kept doing it and next Mom came to the door and found you and said, 'You better stop that or your daddy will find you and give you a whipping.'"

"And I stopped. After all, *you* were the smoker."

We went on and on like that, swapping our little sis/big brother jibes from the past, each one trying to get the last word in. Teasing was still our safest form of affection. It got Roy off the relentless march of declining numbers, and for me, sorrow disguised in the playful words; it erased our distances of years and lives gone different directions. I wanted to talk to Roy about the farm, catch him up on its condition, share the place we'd once dwelled. But most of all, I wanted to save his life.

I thought about how my first love of rocks came from his rock collection. The rocks wouldn't stay put. You were supposed to find rocks, identify them correctly, and place them on a board above their proper name. Our small school had no geology class so the rocks were found, glued down, but then moved. We kept moving them around on the board; they ended up in our pockets, our notebooks, the washing machine. Roy always shared everything with me, even his car he left at home when he went into the navy. I spray painted the interior in black and gold, the school colors, but didn't bother to cover the windows with masking tape. The 1957 Pontiac sported "tinted" windows when he got back, but after the surprise on his face, he only laughed. I think one of the rocks had made its way under the gas pedal.

When I visited him the last time in Katy, he surprised me by showing up along with my nephew at the baggage claim, forty pounds lighter, stooped, on a walker and oxygen, there to meet his sister. He was in such poor health I never expected him to come to the airport. He had on a red jumpsuit and a western straw hat. "Howdy, partner," he drawled, tipping the hat in a teasing salute. I have that image and the faint remains of the wheel ruts left from his search for Elsa on one of those rare rainy Panhandle days. I cherish those marks even though he messed up the road and cut through the native grass—a no-no laid down by my father. They're what I have. That and the peace of our mutual decision—I would buy his part of the farm, money that would help in the ever-escalating cancer expenses for him and his family and a way to ensure the farm stayed intact. And his family, who always welcomes me.

A U.S. Navy vet, he requested no marker, no memorial, and he passed on the option to be buried in the family plot near the farm in Vega. He just wanted to be "buried" at sea, his ashes distributed by the U.S. Coast Guard off the Texas coast.

Which way did the waves roll, Roy? Were you washed back to terra firma, to end up in some stranger's back yard, or farther out, where the shrimp boats go?

CHAPTER EIGHT

Middle Alamosa, Middle Stories

Ysabel's Camp is a sorry sight these days. From a distance the house looks intact, but when Randy and I step up on the creaking porch, we know the adobe has survived only by being covered through the generations of its occupation with wood, siding, tin, and particle board, each now in a state of bleached disarray. The succession of inhabitants has patched and boarded their way through hot summers and snow-packed winters. On the warped mantel over the stone fireplace, the several empty bottles of various rotgut now wedged together in a row of packed dirt say it all. What has been a home and then a cow camp is now merely an abandoned shack, last used for drinking parties. It's not that adobe can't survive. But without the necessary yearly plaster, without someone living there taking care of the place, it is destined to slip away.

This is the culmination of my summers' long hikes. The Middle Alamosa finally spreads out in a large puddle, settling at the river's elevation. After the great drama of its sweeps and moorings, it disappears peacefully and uneventfully among the weeds, bushes, and cattails into the river. To see it only now and not know of its past, the record it has left upstream, is a kind of forgetting. Memory lives in the shapeliness of its narrative.

We poke around. The porch spans the entire front of the house, seven cedar poles supporting the slanted roof. Two abandoned cookstoves sit there like two old-timers whiling away the afternoon; the house is protected in back by canyon walls, caprock-topped, pocked with boulders broken off from above. No tree or much vegetation surrounds the house, just the wild sunflowers that thrive in this

Ysabel's Camp. *Author photo.*

sandy soil. Its two rooms and buckled wooden floors reveal little of
what may have gone on here.

What life is left in the place I find in a scarred back wall. This side
of the house, like the broken windows throughout, is open so that
the layers peeled back by weather and years are down to the original
adobe. A decomposing skeleton, the wall no doubt is from Ysabel's
time, I think—the local mud and straw collected and pressed into
bricks whose order remains. The land yields its skeletons, then takes
them down again. When Frenchy's adobe finally returned to the earth
it came from, near that "boggy creek," Tascosa, people continued to
identify the place by the curved old cottonwood nearby. Here there's a
large boulder out front with grinding holes in it. I'm told it was hauled
in from somewhere else on the ranch to give the place a little character.
We move within places, between places, through places—and places
move, too.

❦ Gayle, "Red," Butch, and I sit as if around a campfire on Gayle's back patio in Albuquerque. The event is friends getting together, simple hamburgers, but served up Gayle-style—thick, not over-cooked, green chile, a fresh salad. We've indulged even knowing that a cobbler awaits. Red is fond of Gayle's peach cobbler; he's been ill, his wife, Gayle's sister, Cherri, is out of town, so she's thoughtfully included him. Butch, Gayle's man friend, always joins us if he's not off hunting or fishing.

Summers on an Albuquerque patio—light breeze, hovering early evening light. Gayle fetches herself another beer and joins us as we try to push back from the table.

Red looks sick. At around seventy, losing weight makes him seem older, fragile. There's something off about his color. He's had some kind of heart flare-up on a trip he and Cherri made to see their daughter and her family in Fort Collins, Colorado. I don't ask, knowing he doesn't want to be the ailing center of attention. He's stoic, wants to push on. Butch, speaking through his voice box due to a tracheotomy years ago, doesn't hesitate to squeak out a vibrating observation. Butch plays the *eirôn*. He and Gayle are good foils for one another in their joking and repartee. I grew up with Gayle and Cherri, classmates of my brother. They babysat me. I also spent long evenings as a child entertaining myself in their bedroom when they were gone, staring at the basketball pennants, the dried corsages from school dances, the cosmetics decking the mirrored vanity. I could smell the hint of their high school lives—the leather basketball letter jackets and face powder sweetening the night air. The smells made me sleepy, and I would climb into the four-poster bed and nap. On these weekends when my parents played bridge with their best friends, the Crouches, the girls were off somewhere at a friend's house or at a school party. The man who leases and manages their farm now still refers to them as "the girls." After Chick died, Virginia became a best friend, too, like my parents. I remember no time when the Crouches—their farm, haystacks, Stinky the big shaggy collie, and the resident geese that would taunt and chase you—weren't part of my life.

I am still the little sis in this circle.

Talk turns to my hikes, and in "talk story" fashion each has a memory of the llano. I'm surprised and pleased by this serendipity, pleased to be talking about the land rather than grousing about the government or some such thing. Butch was reared on a ranch in southern New Mexico, so we share similar ranch memories—Red, too, who moved to Vega as an ag teacher and later married Cherri.

"You remember Roy was my uncle, right?" Gayle reminds us. Roy Turner, she's referring to. "I loved to visit him and Aunt Loula on their ranch right there on the Canadian. Back then you could catch lots of catfish out of the Canadian. He lived near a spring and built a special tank where he put some of the fish so they would grow even larger for good eating. And so we could easily catch them. We gigged the fish and fried them outdoors over an open fire, just like the cowboys cooked, so we wouldn't smell up Aunt Loula's house." I'm thinking Roy must have owned one of the earlier pastores places, built on a creek north of the Canadian. Another beer.

"What I remember about West Texas is the space." Red waves away an offered beer, wades in. "When I was growing up down in West Texas, I would put on my pair of roller skates and tear down what is now I-10—against the traffic." He pauses. We all look at him. "And not meet a single automobile."

We laugh at the prospect of the successful retired lawyer before us, flush-faced, broad-chested, taking off pounds for the wrong reasons, crazy-flying down what now is the busy Pan-American Highway.

"It was that open back then," he adds, and I could see a little of the old Red warming up—rather than the corporate lawyer, here's the red-headed rural kid, a guy who still finds adventure in cowboy stories and is putting together a book about them.

Butch can't sit still long. His voice reverberates from some place deep and far away: "I always liked the quiet of getting out in the country and hunting. I always wanted to kill a bobcat. Just wanted to be able to stalk one and get it. So one day, out west of Socorro, I was hunched down in some sagebrush, just watching, to see what might come up. It was early, just past sunrise, the time you might see the cats. Sure enough, there was a full adult, a big, beautiful female skulking through the sage. It took me a while to get a good look. I raised my gun a couple of times. But there was something weird going on."

Butch, a good storyteller, one who can drag out the point of the story until you're in pain to know it, makes us shift a few times in our seats, delaying a bathroom break—not exactly because of the drama but because we want to get to the end of the story (and maybe get another beer).

Turns out the cat was a mother. She kept looking back over her shoulder and would stop every few steps, making a kind of mewing sound. Butch kept raising the rifle to his shoulder then putting it down, mystified by what the cat was doing. Finally, three kittens emerged from behind the mother. She had been chastising them all the way as they toppled and rolled and frolicked while the mother was trying her best to teach them care and stealth.

"So I wanted to. I sighted the mother cat again. I aimed . . . but I just couldn't shoot."

I thought I heard us collectively exhale, but it might have been only me or my imagination.

"Where's Karen?" I asked, knowing Gayle had also invited her longtime Albuquerque friend from around the block.

"Oh, she just got back from visiting her parents in Minnesota. I picked her up at the airport earlier today. She's bushed but may be over later. Damn that girl. When I tried to help her with her luggage it weighed a ton.

"I said, 'Karen, what the hell? What's in this bag?' She laughed seeing me trying to move the thing and you know what she said? 'Oh, it's just dirt.' DIRT! She brought back dirt from her parents' flower garden. Good rich soil from up there so she can grow some of the same flowers she loves down here."

We all laughed.

Things get moved around. Places move with us.

⅄ Since my mother's death—and Roy's—there were dreams of animals. When my dad died I felt animal visitations, presences. A night heron landed in the elm trees by my house, an unusual visitor to the dry plains and town. Its short neck and hunched, darkened look was like a specter there in the trees at dusk. When I investigated, moving from the porch into the yard, the bird ponderously shifted from tree to tree. I stopped to watch. Why this reminded me of my father, I don't know, but I sensed a restless soul searching for a place to land. The bird finally lofted itself, almost as if reluctant to leave, disappearing northeast into the night sky.

One dream featured a cougar. It's true I had been studying cougars, which were said to be absent now from the Canadian River Valley in Texas. My wildlife biologist friend, Harley Shaw, a spry eighty-year-old who had written the definitive book on cougars and occasionally still worked with graduate students darting and studying them in New Mexico, told me they had been hunted out but also that they might be seen occasionally without establishing a breeding territory here, coming in from New Mexico, up the Canadian canyons.

In the dream I step out of my house into the front yard, where my neighbors, "Frog" and Sandy, are waiting. We all look at the grass and how I have constructed a tiny pen, a green pen, woven of the grass, which they comment on as ecological, protective. Then I look up, the way you do when a shadow passes over your shoulders, the senses responding as if to a predator. There to my right suspended in the sky is a beautiful cougar, just his head visible, but he appears to be frozen in midleap, eyes ablaze, but mouth, rather than shaped in a roar, emitting a permanent scream. The attitude of the body mimics a trophy animal hanging on a wall, but one still animated—living, yet caught in its livingness. Then quickly I am drawn to a crowd in front of me—numbers of people filling a huge stadium. They are jeering, applauding, caterwauling—apparently taunting the suspended cat in all its magnificence trapped in their predatory gaze. The scene feels like one of those horrifying photo ops where people pose, laughing, celebrating, beside the body of someone just hanged.

I wake myself in a howl. The cat—his condition as suspended spectacle—has put "words" in my mouth.

A few months later Randy told me a large male cougar had been shot on the Bridwell Ranch west of Vega. A mule deer, radio collared for study by the Texas Parks and Wildlife, showed up dormant on the computer monitor. Investigating, the ranch manager found evidence that a cougar had taken the deer down and called an "exterminator"—a trapper with dogs trained to tree cougars. In Texas, the cougar—listed as endangered in most of the United States—is officially a varmint and fair game for extermination. The hunter came, the cougar was treed and easily shot out of the tree. Randy reported that the ranch manager showed the photos of the 150-pound male around at church the next Sunday.

Prescient dream? The cougar could have as easily been darted, collared, and studied for his migratory habit into Texas—conserved. The deer population overflows in this state; cougars rarely take cattle, preferring deer. Varmint. What pride is there in displaying a varmint as hunter's bounty?

There was another dream too. In this one I open a door and a cougar head emerges. It is the head of the cat on my mother's body.

The other prominent animal dream was about Elsa, my Weimaraner dog. She strains at her leash as she always did. But this time we are drifting over the Middle Alamosa like two lazy balloons, moving slowly so that I can see the pattern of the creek, the landscape, the expanse of my travels. We begin at Armitage Farms. The sensation is one of floating, being led ever so easily by my dear Elsa over the country I have wanted to see whole. I can see the two draws, where they meet up in the single Middle Alamosa, and the topographic distinctions, where I have hiked, all the way to the river. Elsa is ecstatic, pressing on. I follow her lead as if I am on leash and in joyous wonder. Space and time fold into place.

In yet another dream I'm to feed a crow whose hunger is connected to his silence. His mouth opens; nothing comes out. If I feed him he will talk. Trickster crow, must I keep feeding you? The next day a single crow calls and calls from one of the elms in my yard as I walk in the pasture. Finally he flies over, alone. And the next day there's a singular crow on the outskirts of town, again flying before me as I drive to the farm. Don't crows usually fly in pairs or at least small flocks? What was this crow trying to tell me?

Then there was the dream of the pottery shard that turns into a bird, then flies to become a design in the silver stud of a bridle, where the bit is held in a horse's mouth. There's a kind of aura around the shard.

William Least Heat-Moon writes that you are never really part of a landscape until you dream it.

It's come to the daughter.

⋁ At the county deed office, I relish taking the old books down. Records of Oldham County, from its incorporation in 1881, hold among other things the history of the LS Ranch where Ysabel worked, land sales, cattle and horse brands, including those of Robert Allen Armitage, who purchased one parcel of land in 1929, the other in 1932. The records of the LS and the XIT ranches, the two largest in the Texas Panhandle, show a land swap that preceded my dad's purchase—a swap that led the Landergin brothers, Pat and John, to buy the west LS Ranch in 1904 as well as portions of the XIT. My dad's first job as custodian and junior teller at the First State Bank in Vega was under then president Pat Landergin. I have a photograph of three men—Pat Landergin, Raymond Thompson (later to be bank president), and my dad in the foyer of the bank building, constructed in 1905, a year after Vega became a town. Marble floor, decorative tin ceiling, elaborate hanging lights: the three men seem comfortable in the setting, my dad looking preppy in his shirt and sweater vest.

Dad bought his first farm, the South Place along the Ozark Trail, later Route 66 and now Interstate 40, from the Landergins. After the sale of the LS to the Landergins, Ysabel likely worked for them too. I realize he and Dad had the same bosses.

The county clerk lets me see for myself. Handwritten—in ink pen—the hard-to-read information surfaces slowly as I work through the red leather-bound books. They're ponderous, probably ten pounds apiece, filed along the wall next to an elevated reading table for perusing. No extra weight lifting needed today. I'm looking for the paper trail of deeds for the farm property—documents that prove the Bob and Dorothy ownership, the acquiring of my great-aunt and -uncle's land, the transfer of both to Armitage Farms Corporation—which Dad did for inheritance tax purposes in the 1980s. I like reading the script, which would be such tedious work for many in our computer generation: the words graceful, dancing on the page. Even if hard to read now for our print-accustomed eyes, the scrutiny they demand slows you down, makes you take note of the language and style of the times.

I find the records by first sampling a few of the volumes. Dad purchased the original piece of property for three dollars an acre. I think Mother told me he made ninety dollars a month at the time. Average wages for an LS cowboy in the 1880s were twenty-five dollars a month. Interest rates on farm loans were low, and so Dad paid on the loan most of his life. I looked for the registration of the brands too. Dad registered the Bar R for Roy in 1952, when he was fourteen. This was his way of taking Roy into the farm and cattle business. Me? Each year he let me pick out a calf that was "mine." When sold, he deposited the money in my checking account. At college I received cryptic notes on bank stationery: "Sold calf. Deposited $150.00. Love, Dad." Daddy was a hunt-and-peck guy on the typewriter, no training, and his typing makes it look like the typewriter had the hiccups. I cherished these notes, the closest ever to a letter from my dad. His pride and joy had been a small registered Black Angus herd, which he sold for ten thousand dollars. The farm typically made more money from cattle than farming, but each supplemented the other, the cattle grazing wheat and milo stubble after the harvests, no matter how small.

It—the farm—had come to the daughter. My family, all of them: gone. And I wasn't ready. I never thought of managing the land alone. And I had been the adopted one, a lucky chosen one. What would my father think if he were alive? I often spoke aloud to his vacancy, asking advice, wondering out loud what I should do. The CRP, for example. The Conservation Reserve Program, which allowed you to put your land back in grass. He had passed on it; he wanted the satisfaction of farming, companioned by earth and sky. Me, I jumped at the chance, and the chances were few—bidding on the rate per acre you would be paid to plant grass rather than farm was another form of gambling farmers were familiar with. But I was seriously interested in habitat restoration and I simply couldn't farm the place by myself. So I bid, and after several years I finally got in. As I walked the pastures checking fence, I longed for my dad's firm hand, Roy's enthusiasm, Mother's spunk. A sharing voice to say, You're not crazy, girl. But most of all a *family* farm. Now there was only the land to hold me. I needed its adoption.

⅄ The last farmer to lease the land after my dad's death was gone too; before the farm was put in CRP I found another young man, Lucas, whose father was known for his sometimes unconventional (read "conservation-minded") but savvy and very successful farming practices. I assumed Lucas would follow. I wanted someone who would steward the place, get as close to sustainable agriculture as possible. On a dry-land farm and with the plethora of farm programs, this was like asking the LS cowboys to continue working for low pay through drought, blizzards, and heel flies. When Lucas first toured the place all he could comment on was the scurrilous bindweed, something I felt responsible for. Years of leasing the land had allowed it to get out of hand. His dad had all but eradicated bindweed on their place. My dad had, too, when he had run the farm himself. It took vigilance, being on a place all the time. I felt guilty as we drove through the fields, beautiful to me, but the most visible living thing that early fall was the bindweed. Had I, in the necessity of my distant university employments, turned into that "suitcase farmer," the one whose stewardship may be compromised by not being on the land?

The pasture at first continued under the cattle lease of Tuff Harwell, who had leased the grass from Dad for over forty years. My brother, showing occasional big brother protectiveness, exclaimed when at one point I told him that Tuff and I were dating, "But he was the wildest boy in Vega High School!" What that meant for early 1950s I didn't ask. "But Roy, that was back then. He—we—are grown up now." True, Tuff exhibited a lifestyle I wasn't used to. He picked me up for dates in his brand new elegantly grey Lincoln Continental, two scotch and waters conveniently waiting in attached tumblers on the back of the front seats. But now Tuff was getting older. He married and moved to his ranch northwest of Adrian. Running more cattle on our place from that distance didn't interest him. So Sam, his brother-in-law, took over the grass. Now I had two men in my life again who would stop along the county roads and talk for a while, including Lucas, whose sensitivity, smarts, and warmth helped me feel part of an extended family again.

But each time something got settled at the farm, something else popped up. When the wind energy representative contacted me I wasn't ready for that, either. I didn't want the turbines. Now, even more than before, I needed my meditative walks, the draws, the beloved ever-grounding landscape lines. Wasn't it Husserl who said: "Every experience has its own horizon"? I had to learn, like Dad fruitlessly trying to stem the Middle Alamosa flow: places continually change. There's no keeping them.

The particular horizon of this new experience spanned countless documents, contracts made and revised, endless meetings with the Cielo representative, consultations with lawyers, phone calls to neighbors, meetings with engineers, discussions with county officials. The miasma of wind energy company processes became a constant disturbance—countless revised documents, a stream of estoppels—and I resisted every step of it while simultaneously having to maintain a vigilance about contractual matters. Fronting this horizon in my mind was the image of marching turbines, the reality that they would now dominate the landscape, perhaps impact wildlife, and worse, change the natural beauty, the natural genius, of that lyric land forever.

The first thing to go was my privacy. The county road, once only caliche and wonderfully winding, flanked in summer by the tall wildflowers, ironweed, Queen Anne's lace, and antelope horn with its supple stalks and waving puckers of seed hearts, was to be straightened, widened, and "made better." What more could a landowner want, the engineers and managers asked me, than a perfectly straight and wider road, paved with gravel? To build this initial road, for at least six months there was an endless parade of huge trucks bearing gravel, dirt, and water. Earthmovers roved up and down from sunup to sundown. There was no time I could walk anymore unless I wanted to go out there at midnight. When I did go out, I was stopped by a security guard who worked for the construction company.

"Hello, ma'am." Nod. "What are you doing out here?"

I'm walking, which should be evident. "I'm just walking. I own this land," gesturing, motioning toward something, that elusive horizon of mine.

Blank look. Disbelief? Older woman in worn-out sneakers, shorts, frayed tee-shirt. Sure.

Long pause. "Okay. But be careful."

Disgusted nod.

I felt under surveillance every time I went to the farm. My favorite Big Brother experience was the tracking by the local sheriff's department deputy—a new guy who didn't know me. I could see him from the mile and a half turn-around on the county road, right before you turn to go to the North Place. He pulled behind my old truck, sat there. He was running the numbers, checking me out. This happened more than once, with different deputies. One time he came down the road to meet me and ask—again—what I was doing. Once he waited and chastised me when I arrived back at the truck. "Do you realize you have left your purse in an unlocked vehicle?" I started to tell him the front door no longer locked, but just let it go. I knew he was just doing his job.

And so for a while, as the number of trucks increased—now that the roads accessing the wind turbines were also being built—I quit going.

I couldn't bear to watch it. The creation of human-altered space, the monumentality of technology against the fragile grasses and remembered earth. The blotting-out of a place once holding nothing but open space—no evidence (except for the fences and a couple of windmills) of human scurrying. Now where the antelope had borne babies the summer before—eight heads barely visible above the wheat stubble line (and the same color)—there was nothing. Gone.

Meanwhile, the contracts marched on. The Austin-based wind power company, Cielo, contracted all the land, then sold the leases, smartly staying on then as builders—an intelligent move for a small company. There was cleverness all around. Neighboring ranchers— my generation—once stubborn about their land, became advocates of the wonders of wind power. And why not? Each stood to make a flat rate of an estimated twenty thousand dollars a year per turbine, plus a percentage of the profit from the electricity generated, with yearly increases. The wind projects east and west of Vega totaled approximately 244 turbines. The county touted the project as an economic boom for everyone in the county, even though the majority of the new jobs came from the outside. Supposedly after ten years, the average citizen would see tax reductions because of the company's investment. Men whose land was impacted made comments like this one from Tom Henry Green: "I've got to think about my kids and grandkids. Besides they're putting the turbines on the south side of the ranch. We can't see them from the ranch house." *But I can, Tom Henry.* Cielo seemed to be dealing mainly with the large landowners—more profit for everyone, less hassle. The little guys were, well, little guys.

And one gal.

Neighbor Kim Montgomery, who was perhaps the most meticulous and insightful of the ranchers in his dealings (even making multiple trips to Austin to check on things), also made sure in his contract that the turbines didn't compromise the land near his house or the old spring site where the family picnicked. But then just a few years later he moved to Amarillo. Now only one of the ranches nearby has a family living on it. Out of sight, out of mind.

And the turbines kept coming. The Spinning Spur Project cut near Milkweed, the large playa that was a sustaining landmark for prehistoric and historic travelers. They came west, through Green's, into Montgomery's, and through the Bush property I leased between my two places. (Of course the leaser got nothing, just the added difficulty of plowing and planting around the turbines and the almost two-year disturbance due to construction time.) I couldn't bear seeing the native grass grated out, replaced by a huge road (they had to be wide enough to transport the turbines), and watching an enormous culvert collect weeds and debris—clog up—right on the drainage into Green's canyons, a primary drainage into the Middle Alamosa Creek. Just up from where Dad tried to shore up the erosion before he died, the engineers had unwittingly built something that would stop the flow. And they constructed the eighty-meter-tall turbines exactly where my favorite view of the draws and Green's canyon was. I wondered, did the construction workers ever notice this view?

I contacted the county judge, Donnie Allred, the chief local contact (and advocate) about the road building on the South Draw county road. I felt ridiculous—and was—sitting in his upscale office with western memorabilia touches, discussing the migration of monarchs. They feed primarily on native wildflowers and lay eggs only in milkweed, I submitted. If the road takes out part of the bar ditch, it will destroy the native feeding and reproduction routes. Monarchs are more or less endangered, at least always at risk. He smiled. Don't worry; the road won't be that wide. And if they raise the road, I continued? When it rains, the water will back up into the draw, causing even more erosion. I even brought photographs to document what the Middle Alamosa running after a rainstorm looked like. To Donnie's credit he actually drove out to the farm and took a look.

The photos were hard for anyone to believe because we were, still are, in a drought. Mostly the draw stayed dry. When the dust cleared, literally, the county road was not that damaging and mercifully the engineers had not put in a culvert there. But the North Place was ruined for me. Six turbines covered the Bush property I leased. A line of twelve turbines farther north on Green's completely hemmed in my land. As far as you could see east and west were turbines. Scharbauer's Ranch to the northwest got approximately forty-three turbines. Armitage Farms: zero.

I was surrounded. Even on the South Place, when I walked down in that draw, curious as to whether there was any place on the farm that was free of their dominance, I could see the tips of the turbines turning. They were like ballerinas, all graceful spin. But so foreign. In a land so undeveloped that the sky was velvet black to the north at night, no house lights or microwave towers present, now there was the intermittent blinking of eighty-seven red lights—and more to come. The turbines followed the contour of the breaks, like the hawks before them, taking advantage of the uplifts. Here was the modern demarcation of the land's mysterious and secretive contours. A human demystifying of the surprise and silence I reveled in. There was no escape. The turbines defined our new horizons.

In the lawyer's meetings over the contracts, no one raised any environmental questions. Except me. Stares all around. "What about plans to remove the turbines," I asked, "if the technology becomes dated?"

"Dynamite, I guess," one of the experts hazarded. Outside of each landowner trying to get a deal that protected whatever he valued, no mention was made of possible impact on birdlife, the antelope migrations, or certainly "aesthetics." Who was speaking for nature? Certainly I supported "green" industry, but research had begun to show that wind farms were not without environmental impact. Estimates were that 33,000 to 111,000 bats would be killed by turbines by 2020; 75,000 to 270,000 birds per year, including 80 golden eagles. In winter conditions when there is ice forming on the blades, the chemical used to de-ice could pollute ground water and is toxic to cattle, fish, and local food sources. The wind farms can impact weather conditions; the wind turbulence caused by the blades creating a drying phenomenon, raising temperatures up to two degrees at night, adding to evaporation and possibly impacting the potential for rain. All this in an already drought-stricken and progressively more arid area. All this for a possible 2–3 percent contribution to energy consumed in this country. And, let's be honest, for me the turbines ruined my meditative walks, the space and place that harbored me. Wasn't I as entitled to that harvest as those buying the wind?

In typical Texan fashion, there was some unspoken trust in the wisdom of the establishment, in this case what the lawyers, the wind energy company, and the local media assured. No one questioned an economic development that would make many of the landowners in the area even richer and was supposedly nonpolluting. It was a win-win situation.

⌄ I kept holding a vision before me, memory a kind of mirage. In it Genneil Curphey, another of my hiking buddies who had accompanied Randy, Lisa, and me to Little Arrowhead Peak, were walking the old creek bed north of Tom's camp. She specialized in wildflower identification, and I kept close behind, listening to her musings over one plant or another: "Tansy aster? Or, or . . . ?"

We came upon a webbing of sorts, but like a translucent wall, and stopped suddenly to avoid entanglement. It was about three feet across and suspended between rank weed stalks. At first we thought it was a spider web, all building up and creation. Then we sensed it was something in its last stages, delicate, decomposing.

"What's this?" Genneil asked, tipping her straw hat back in order to bend more closely.

The filaments danced in the wind, buoyed this way and that, catching the afternoon light, billowing shadows.

"I think this may be the skin of something, no, I mean—look—just the hair. What's left," I said reaching out but not touching." Maybe the last stages of some animal—a coyote?"

Shape-shifter. Trickster. Death is like that.

I was filled with wonder, fear, and the desire to take care of.

It was the feeling I had trying to take care of Mother. The fragility, the threads that barely hung on. One misstep and. . . . And now that feeling about the land, and the turbines too.

"Whatever it is, it will go to the loving embrace of Mother Earth," Genneil said.

We hovered there, perhaps a moment just before the skein's vacancy
would fill the air.
"We'll buy your wind," the Cielo representative had said.
But the breath of the story is not for sale.

⋁ I know my situation is extremely unusual. I never expected to make
a living from the farm or its transformations. I had a separate career,
and the land meant something very different to me. What I wanted
was to restore habitat—and then to let the land be. My modest attempt
at habitat restoration—contributing to a continuity of the plains as
wildlife corridors—countered the upright turbines, but now my project could never really be finished. There would always be the ongoing
disturbances: roads resurfaced, turbines checked, repaired, serviced.
The North Draw grass along the turbine road was scraped clean; the
drainage they had constructed, full of debris. It seemed there were
always men out there now checking me out as if I didn't belong.

To be able to walk it, in peace, to care for it, to witness its little
surprises. *Want to go to the farm?* I pursued that goal through the
farm plan that allowed for conversion of cropland to grass. Grass.
Yes, even in my time, there had been nighthawks, curlews, hawks,
occasional eagles, antelope, meadowlarks, and south of my place even
a few prairie chickens. Before, the land—with only three of us landowners and no beehive of men, trucks and cranes—had sat, mostly
keeping to its own rhythms.

The wind farm company widened roads, bridging the North Draw
with a huge culvert shortening the distance between turbines on
my neighbor's property. Would I find myself, like my dad years ago,
down in the draw, only rather than shoring up the sides, cleaning
out the culvert to restore the flow? The process and road took out
quite a bit of native vegetation. There was an agreement to restore the
grass, but it never happened. The bald land blew in the dry springs
and summers and the building debris left along the roadway created
a permanent bump that made the original farm roads it crossed
almost unusable. It was very difficult to get to the north windmill or
the north fields. These changes destroyed the little ribbon road Sam
had etched through the years that followed the hillock shape, a series
of curves to abate any erosion, in rhythm with the land's natural

contours. It had always been a cardinal point of my dad's to leave the lightest human print possible on the place. No cutting across the native prairie, no unneeded tracks. Something about the bulldozed prairie seemed against nature. I wanted to continue to feel part of its cycles, not the opposite.

Another contract—this time for transmission towers for the next stage of the project. No. I didn't want them either. This time they would be on the South Place. I would not only be surrounded; I would be occupied.

Back to the lawyer's. "Shelley, if you don't take the money, they'll just move across the fence onto your neighbor's. You'll still have the eyesore. But you won't have the money. Don't be silly."

I sign.

My reasoning? The money will enable me to pay for the CRP and its maintenance, one habitat restored as the other is lost.

The Cielo projects *are* impressive. These are some of the largest turbines in North America. Projects Spinning Spur I, II, and III encompass 244 turbines stretching east of Wildorado to west of Adrian. Spinning Spur II—the 87 wind turbines built around the breaks near the Middle Alamosa—services sixty thousand homes, encompasses 28,426 acres of land near Vega. It's a 161-megawatt facility; it costs $1 million per megawatt of capacity to build. EDF Renewable Energy, a subsidiary of EDF Energies Nouvelles, based in France, and Google, now own the facility. The electricity is managed by the Electric Reliability Council of Texas, which services households in 75 percent of the state, none of them in the Texas Panhandle.

Like water projects in Roberts County in the eastern Panhandle, through which water is purchased and delivered downstate, the energy of the "high lonesome" of the Texas Panhandle for now is going outward.

And what of the spirits of place—like the essence of those disappeared pronghorns? Do they stay? Regroup? Must we reimagine them?

Of the many peoples who populated the llano and breaks areas for the past twelve thousand years—Clovis mammoth hunters, Archaic hunters and gatherers, early agricultural village dwellers, Plains Indians, buffalo hunters, pastores, cowboys, cattle ranchers, irrigation farmers, feed-lot and dairy economies, oil and gas, sand and gravel, and now "green energy" interests—each reacted to the same space by creating different places. But as Elliott West argues, the fundamental energy of the plains—grass—has been harvested, beginning with prehistoric life into buffalo, horses (the Comanche and Kiowa), cattle, and more recently with the technological uses of the related energies of water, wind, and soil. Without exception, each of these industries traded the basic resource energy of the plains outward, building networks of trade and complex economies. The scarcity of the replacement or sustainable energy flowing in hastens the need for counties like Oldham to seize the turbine days. Inconsistent farming economies, especially on these plains, leads to the decimation of small towns. People leave. So these places are often defined by "use" rather than by any sense of interrelationship. Spirits of place and an individual's sense of place may prove oppositional rather than complementary.

Ⓥ The Middle Alamosa has only the "middle" generation to sense its spirits now. That generation may still have some contact, through memory of an older generation's experiences and interactions with place. Stories may cross and connect, like the time I spoke with Hotdog McKendrie's daughter, Teresa, asking her about her father's experiences out on the LS and at Ysabel's Camp.

In the front room of her farmhouse north of Vega—a room containing memorabilia of her dad's cowboy days: a saddle, photographs, a scruffy old Stetson—she handed me a transcribed copy of his recollections, "Winter at Ysabel's Camp," written in 1946.

"One of the strangest things that happened to Daddy out there," she said, "was the appearance of a strange man, a kind of wild man, who showed up at the house one day. Daddy and Hank Ruhl, who was cowboying there at that time too, took him in, fed him, and then he disappeared by the next morning. Daddy said he never spoke, was dressed in tattered clothes. They had no idea where he'd come from, how he was living out in a winter like that.

"And then I remembered that when I was a girl we were at a picnic closer into town, down in the breaks on Green's. You know, what we used to call 'the Picnic Grounds.' I had gone off to use the bathroom out in the brush near some caves. Something made me look up and I saw a man, just fleetingly, dash out of one cave and disappear into the brush. It kind of frightened me all these years until I listened to Daddy's story and wondered whether that was the same 'wild' man."

I must find more of these middle stories before their tellers are gone. Such stories may serve as a common ground shared in a culture based primarily on the individual, private ownership, and the commerce of use.

The spirits of place may be ghosts, or they may be shamans. Historian Daniel Flores in his "Alternate Worlds: Comanche Sense of Place and the Pre-Agricultural Llano Estacado" connects Comanche petroglyph sites with their sacred places, places that, as anthropologist Dan Gelo says, are honored not because of the physical place only but because in that place it is possible to receive the spirit donors. The Comanche referred to the llano—the flat "empty" plains—as Nimiahti, without people. They mostly avoided such areas, preferring the streams and rivers, the high prominences—cliffs, mountains, mesas. Deep narrow canyons were avoided, thought to be inhabited by ghosts, but wide canyons, like the Palo Duro, were favored for openness, good camp grounds. Contrastingly, for the Kiowa, the narrow canyon slits could be the places for the return of the buffalo. Flores clarifies that his conception of the spirits of place is not one of "supernatural entities or qualities" but of "essential and activating possibilities to the inspiration that real slices of the tangible world can impart." The rock art sites near springs, like the Bison Run with the shaman figures encircling the solution cavities, suggest that these activating and tangible possibilities—water, food, shelter, beliefs—are necessary for a continuance of one's culture, hence sacred. The land itself and the stories tell us how to live.

Comanche and other indigenous peoples have always mapped such places through stories—memories that link places with history and experience. Perhaps to hold a place in one's memory is a repeated return to what is the most human need of all: feeling emplaced. The field of study called "biophilia" posits that certain kinds of landscapes may attract us as a result of our evolutionary past. This may explain the peculiar and mysterious déjà vu we experience at times. Once I felt compelled—in the blur of an instant—to look to my left while walking in a park for exercise one day. What I saw was the humped back of a bear, loping alongside. This all in a moment, but distinct as if I were seeing the creature in another time period. The ancestral may be linked to essential forms of place; the contemporary as well. Some scientists argue that certain electromagnetic fields may vibrate through cliffs or mountain ranges, affecting human moods, encouraging affinities.

But, Flores reminds us, for the Comanche, mapping involved an intimate knowledge of places by deeply inhabiting them. Twentieth- and twenty-first-century movement, which marks most of our lives, let alone the commerce of these prairies, allows little time for or emphasis on "dwelling." In 1875, around the time Ysabel and other pastores moved into the Panhandle, Jacob Sturm, a military aide, accompanied to the Oklahoma reservation the last band of Comanches to surrender to the U.S. military. The group moved from the vicinity of Big Spring to Fort Sill, Oklahoma, and along the way Sturm was privileged to record the Comanches' names and some stories of significant places in Comancheria. Places were not named for individuals but mostly from sensory understanding, and often keyed to a particular event in Comanche history. Wov-aha-tah-honovit, for example, Gelo translates as "woman vagina spy on /look for river" and Sabe-Honovith, pointed out by both Quanah Parker and Isatai as a favorite, as "a good-place-to-camp-with-cottonwoods-and-springs." The group described the caprock area upon which the Llano Estacado expands as "an island, surrounded by rivers"—the later Anglo explorers' "sea of grass"—perhaps the single descriptive connection shared by Native dwellers and Anglo immigrants alike, only where one saw a sheltering island, the other saw a forbidding sea.

In 1999, a Comanche elder, Carney Saupitty, reiterated in a talk in Arlington, Texas, the necessity of immersion in a place in order to sense its spirit. By immersion only could stories then perpetuate the spirits of place. In his recounting cultural memories of fighting the Spanish, fleeing Mackenzie's troops, his stories were full of remembered places, places passed along through stories, *but not ones he had directly experienced*. Of the bordering rivers of the Llano Estacado, one river, Ysa-hono, Wolf River (the Canadian), figured into a key Comanche / Cheyenne / Arapaho battle fought nearby. He remembered Tucumcari Mountain, about seventy miles west of Vega, as

"Food Peak" or "Hunter's Point" because it allowed the Comanche to scout the buffalo. *Tukamakaru* is a Comanche word meaning "to lie in wait for someone or something to approach." Flores concludes that the Comanche remembered llano topography as a conception not of one world, but of two, "Red Badlands" and "Top-of-the-Badlands." The Red Badlands were what is today called Caprock Canyonlands, southeast of the Canadian Breaks, a place Saupitty associated with campsites, sanctuary, and power. Top-of-the-Badlands connotes food (buffalo) but is devoid of people and sacrality. Today that area ironically is the center of the Panhandle's primary populations, agricultural empire, and ambitious oil, gas, and wind energy development; once devoid of people, now it is the place of commercial immersion.

The Kwahadas, or Antelope Band, those last Comanches to be brought onto the reservation by Sturm and his troops, had retreated in the mid-1860s to that wildest country along the edges of the Staked Plains, the Canadian Breaks and its canyons. Like their namesakes, these were fleet and ingenious survivors, and they knew intimately the relationship between the flat and canyon lands and their place in them. They appeared to live along the edges of this world, disappearing and reappearing like a mirage, the draws, like those on Armitage Farms where I still find occasionally their flint points, an entry into highways, the continuities of sustenance and protection.

When I see the pronghorns at the farm, I always think of them, the Kwahadas. But I think mostly of the miraculous continuity of DNA and how place is a gathering phenomenon. *Antilocapra americana*, commonly called antelope, is the last of twelve antilocaprid species that existed during the Pleistocene period, some 2.6 million years ago. With the advent of humans in North America, about five of the species survived. Now the pronghorn map the longest migrations in North America, some traveling 160 miles overland; their range is from Canada to Mexico through most western and southwestern states. They were endangered by the 1920s, their numbers reduced to only thirteen thousand, but conservation efforts have boosted their populations to an estimated five hundred thousand to 1 million. Three subspecies remain endangered.

I thrill to see them, usually six to twelve together, a modest mixed-sex herd in winter and in spring mostly females, with an

Pronghorn at Armitage Farms. *Author photo.*

occasional bachelor male off by himself in his solitary life. They breed
in September, with fawns born in late May. Newborn fawns spend
their first twenty to twenty-six days hiding in vegetation. When the
first road excavations for the wind farm began, a small herd of females
and fawns at first kept to their tawny places in the ripening wheat
fields, only their heads visible as the rumbling trucks and trailing dirt
railed by. Checking fence one day at the farm, Sam said he jumped a
fawn and her mother, startled from the high kochia weeds along the
fencerow. The doe escaped—with speeds up to fifty miles per hour they
can outrun any of their natural enemies—but the fawn instinctively lay
back down, even though by then they both were exposed to man and
horse and to any predator, cougar, coyote, or bobcat that happened by.

Even on foot, I can only get so close, and when I see them, white buff
rump the only giveaway in their dusky butterscotch coats dissolving, I
slow and stop, squinting into the distance to observe. These moments
of stillness are ensured by the pronghorns' own looking—with their
eyes prominent and high on the head they can see up to a distance of
three miles. I am held in the stillness of this gaze, the moment before

they may bolt. If I can be still, empty my buzzing head, then we are connected, if only for a minute, in a shared sense of absolute being. Eckhart Tolle writes in *Stillness Speaks* about the experience of nature in this way: "When you perceive nature only through mind, through thinking, you cannot sense its aliveness, its beingness. You see the form only and are unaware of the life within the form—the sacred mystery. Thought reduces nature to a commodity to be used in the pursuit of profit or knowledge or some such utilitarian purpose. The ancient forest becomes timber, the bird a research project, the mountain something to be mined or conquered."

As antelope and I stare, I imagine a dialogue with Tolle.

"Pronghorns have hollow hairs. In winter, when their coat may be cold and wet, this allows them a shield to the cold," I begin.

"Watch an animal, a flower, a tree and see how it rests in Being. It is itself. It has enormous dignity, innocence, and holiness. However, for you to see that, you need to go beyond the mental habit of naming and labeling. The moment you look beyond mental labels, you feel that ineffable dimension of nature which cannot be understood by thought or perceived through the senses. It is a harmony, a sacredness that permeates not only the whole of nature but is also within you."

"Pronghorns primarily eat forbs, shrubs, and grasses. Cacti can also provide as much as 40 percent of their diet," I continue.

"Have you allowed that familiar yet mysterious being we call plant to teach you its secrets? Have you noticed how deeply peaceful it is? How it is surrounded by a field of stillness? The moment you become aware of a plant's emanation of stillness and peace, that plant becomes your teacher."

"Pronghorn horns are composed of a slender blade of bone that grows from the frontal bones of the skull. A keratinous sheath covers the bony core and is shed and regrown annually," I offer.

"You are not separate from nature. We are all part of the One Life that manifests itself in countless forms throughout the universe, forms that are completely interconnected. When you recognize the sacredness, the beauty, the incredible stillness and dignity in which a flower or animal exists, you add something to that flower or animal. Through your recognition, your awareness, nature too comes to know itself."

Silence.

"Thinking is a stage in the evolution of life. Nature exists in innocent stillness that is prior to the arising of thought. The tree, the flower, the bird, the rock are unaware of their own beauty and sacredness. When human beings become still, they go beyond thought. There is an added dimension of knowing, of awareness, in the stillness that is beyond thought."

Silence.

"Nature can bring you to stillness. That is its gift to you. When you perceive and join with nature in the field of stillness, that field becomes permeated with your awareness. That is your gift to nature."

Antelope and I are locked in this knowing until I turn and go back. I can't help it. I am thinking how the turbine construction across the West necessitated research to see if the pronghorn migration and habits would be interrupted. We all understand that habitat loss and fragmentation are the greatest threats to the natural world.

It seems Antelope and I have found our way back home among the turbines after all—and the transmission lines. I discovered by following their tracks that they'd smartly come up the Middle Alamosa Creek bed as if it were a planned wildlife corridor; the line of turbines broke there, resuming on the other side. They found the one route not crossed by the turbines. I'll never get used to the parade of men in trucks still casing the country, roads to be maintained, turbines repaired. But we've returned through the Middle Alamosa to the draws in this habit of landscape.

Deeply inhabit.

"Habit" and "habitat" are wrapped in their Middle English origins. "Habitat" in the Latin means "it dwells" and was used in the Latin descriptions of plant and animal species in old natural histories. "Habit," from the Latin, means "to have, to hold." One definition of "dwell" is to fasten one's attention.

Our propensity is to name, to hold, to control the natural energies of these plains.

But I know better. We are held by them, in place.

The Suspended Pool

"Did I tell you I found out more about Ysabel?"

If Randy was listening it was hard to tell. He was intent upon the severe grade that even his Ford 150 struggled to make.

"I had an e-mail from a gal at the Historical Society of Guadalupe County. You know, Anton Chico. Where Ysabel grew up." I had my hands on the dash, holding myself against the surge upward. My voice warbled with the jerks of the pickup over the rocky road.

"Hmmmm."

"She researched the birth records at the church there and gave me a birth date that is later than the one on his stone out at the cemetery. That earlier date was on the death certificate Doc Lloyd signed and Hondo, his brother, witnessed. Ysabel wasn't as old as I thought. Born in 1859."

"Hmmmm. Hey I need to stop for a ciggy."

I was a little irritated with Randy's distractions, but after all, the truck was lurching up the escarpment, and we couldn't see over the top. We could very well reach it and pitch down into a gulley or deep canyon. He parked precariously with the nose of the truck pointed upward. Smokers have got to have their drag. And I couldn't complain. At home my own addiction awaited: oatmeal cookies, lots of them. I'd learned to expect the unexpected of Randy. Like another time when he skidded to a stop at the bottom of an arroyo, spotting an appealing large rock that he immediately abandoned the pickup for, perching himself there like a thin Buddha, arms gracefully extended outward, fingers up in a meditative pose. "Energy place," he'd told me.

"Hey look."

He was also extremely observant.

There before us in the sandstone surface was a series of grinding holes, some filled with telltale grassy knobs, like some willful Archie comics haircut, and there, in front of them, in what appeared to be a deep sandstone basin, a pool of water.

We were up top an escarpment. Deep canyons lay off to the sides below. This was a surprising place to find water, this high up, and in a basin.

We looked around. Iridescent indigo dragonflies, like miniature flags, hovered among the random grass stems jutting from the reddish water. The red clay, so pervasive in this part of the Middle Alamosa drainage, seemed to color everything. It was getting toward evening and the last sunlight brightened the waters—red and blue, red and blue.

We noted a very deep canyon ahead—down below the basin— which, like so many in the breaks, gave no warning, simply plummeted below us. After exploring the grinding holes and the area—and discovering some flint—we trailed around the edge of the canyon, thinking to get a view from the other side. When we did, we fell silent.

Across the way, in the lingering dusk, the pool, so solid, wedged into the hard sandstone cliff, revealed itself to be suspended. A bare, curved rock bottom was all that held it from collapsing to the canyon floor. The cliff face beneath it had apparently eroded away leaving the precariously held waters above.

What was it? Surely not a springs. But it could be. The waters seemed to attract life, grass sprouts, some cane, weeds of course, and the dragonflies glowing as if in a Japanese painting. If not springs, then what. A plunge pool? Likely. But still. There had been no rain in weeks. Evaporation is around 70 percent in this semi-arid country. And the winds. The daily average is sixteen miles an hour. Yet here is water and the grinding holes to suggest, yes, it could be or could have been springs. Native folks had worked here. It could be an old seepage.

"About Ysabel?" It was Randy. We had both been so quiet I almost forgot he was there.

"Oh. Yeah, I guess there's no way of recovering any reliable stories."

"You just have to make them up!"

"Well. I mean one source has him part of a murder as a young boy, but the source inaccurately names his father as involved. He was not even in this area, but back in Anton Chico. And there are other mistakes in the source. So I don't trust it. At least the way it's reported. And you know the other one—that patronizing description of him in the Oldham County History book, something like 'for a Mexican'—wasn't he Hispano?—'he was a pretty good cowboy and didn't cause no trouble.' At least Dulce Sullivan in her book on the LS includes the Stetson hat story and notes he was a long-time, highly regarded cowboy. That sort of thing!"

"But I thought you had a lead on his family—a cousin, or a nephew, something like that?"

"Yeah." By this time we'd eased back into the pickup, Randy had had another cigarette, and we were going over that hill no matter what. "But that was a dead end. I did talk to Salvador Gurule, a great-great nephew, who steered me toward two aunts he thought might know something about Ysabel. One was supposed to be in Pueblo, Colorado, but I couldn't track her down, no phone number. She supposedly is in her nineties. And the other lady I actually phoned in Clovis. She said she married into the family and didn't know anything about Ysabel. Her husband would, but he's deceased."

"Bummer."

"Yes," I thought. "I sought the arc of my dad's and Ysabel's story and found—what?—a prairie. A prairie becoming breaks." Like the spirit line in old Zuni pots, which runs to the heart of the animal, connecting hunter to reverenced prey, an arc shaped not only by memory or time, but of shifting place. *Place, our teacher, sacred because of what has happened there: the kinship of all living things and their stories, root of a universal spirit available to those sensitive to its movements.*

I was thinking of the one story I had found in all this searching that might be an oral link through time between my dad and Ysabel. Ruth Haliburton, an old friend from the bank years, told me a story that my dad had told her his dad had told him about what "a Mexican" had told him. It was a story that consoled me too, about the turbines and their minions—providing comic relief and a reason for them being here.

"Your grandfather had just moved from Arkansas," Ruth had said, "and was asking if there were any cyclones here. I think that's what they called tornadoes then."

I'd nodded, remembering one of my elementary texts with the folk hero "Cyclone Bill," who swept across the country in a spinning whirl of dust.

"Anyway, he said the Mexican said, 'No, no cyclones. But the straight wind, it blows like hell.'"

I'll always believe that "Mexican" was Ysabel.

⇂ I started to tell Randy the story, but we were headed up now, and I knew enough of Randy's love of a carnival ride via truck in the breaks to grab the dash and catch my breath before it was too late. But when he reached the top, he pulled over onto a level area at mesa top. There before us, rising like some apparition, was an oil station, the black grasshopper-looking machine churning. The second big surprise of the day.

"What the hell."

"Damn it. They're everywhere, these oilies. Roads, derricks. How many of these does a fella need to have a good living? And what's that?" Randy pointed at a large, black hose that snaked back down the escarpment right to the pool's edge.

"Is that pumping water out?" I asked, incredulously.

"Or," Randy added, "something in?"

I thought of the sand and gravel pits, how they scarred the land, removing whole mesas, destroying the natural drainage. The topo maps rightfully called them "strip mining." And I remembered that another property owner had released feral pigs for hunting on his land. They had spread up the tributaries, persistent, destructive.

And now this.

Stunned again and a little heartbroken that our fragile miracle was compromised either way, we were quiet for a while. I realized the suspended pool represented everything about my Middle Alamosa quest. For a moment, the flow of stories and memories were held— but they were not just "pristine" nature, they were infused with God-knows-what from the oil rigs too—momentary until they slip away, drained, evaporated. It was those moments I'd sought to apprehend,

The Suspended Pool. *Author photo.*

puzzle together like the broken pottery shards, a lost vocabulary strewn among stones.

I thought about how Robert Adams, the "new topographics" photographer, redefines beauty in our contemporary world of altered "nature." He would understand the ambiguity of such a pool. In his photographs of encroaching housing developments along the Colorado North Range, he creates a visual equipoise. In black and white, the mountain, shadowed foreground, and overexposed sky reveal also the contour of the marching houses, seemingly part of the natural world. This is today's beauty, this surprising angle of repose. In mining, an angle of repose is the moment a stone ceases to roll down a hillside. In Adams's photos, in the llano, it's the moment we perceive beauty as the equipoise of the natural and altered landscape. I think: beauty must be learning to look without judgment. And being is not stasis, but the constant embracing of change.

"So there *is* one Ysabel story I trust," I said. "The historical society gal said Ysabel's record was hard to find at first because when he was christened the clerk recorded him as a girl."

"What?" Randy had reached the top, and sure enough below lay a route that might rival the ride of a Coney Island roller coaster.

"Yeah, and she said, despite the mistake, she was sure this was Ysabel. 'You know, sometimes the priests had a little too much of the communion wine,' she said."

We laughed, dispelling sadness if only for a moment. Like the suspended pool, momentary, fragile, reservoir of memory, the storied summers.

Randy looked over, and I knew what was next. We would plunge down the hill. I would suppress a silly scream, and he would gun the motor. For an instant, we had that view—the broad Canadian valley before us, spread out in its late summer greens, rouged purples. It was a breathless sight, just like the first time I saw it from afar on Armitage Farms.

⛰ On the way back, late evening hues settling in, Randy pointed out the direction of the farm (I never learned to say "my farm"; never will)—something we enjoyed doing. Now there were the lights of the turbines we didn't need, didn't want, to guide us. The red blinking lights of the seventy-plus turbines rimmed the night sky, interrupting the deep ink-black sky of my childhood. Something of the native wildness had been taken out of the country, so domesticated by its wires, towers, crosshatching roads, sand and gravel mining—and out of us too. But still I returned—and will.

Just the day before, on my daily trip to the farm, I'd found a single deer antler near the fence where I'd first crossed over all those years ago. *We create the continuities, we do.* I thought of it as the antler of my first guide, the mule deer, who had so delicately picked his way to the canyon floor, giving me a way. Perhaps he had come and gone—and come again.

Next early morning, I had a dream in that lucid period around four o'clock. There was a blank white page and across it, rather than words, there were tracks. Red tracks, probably deer tracks. They seemed random rather than purposeful as they angled across the page. Then a shadow seemed to come down, like a hand trying to put a fence around the tracks. There was a voice. "Let them go," it said.

Acknowledgments

To my writing friends who steadfastly supported this project by not only closely critiquing this book but loving it: Zita Arocha, Ann Coberly, Michelle Potter, Pat Hickman, Ani King, and Bill Tydeman—thank you all. And especially you, Gail Hovey, who carefully read and questioned and shared.

Special thanks to friend and hiking buddy Genneil Curphey: your appreciation of the plains and encouragement throughout this project kept me moving forward.

Folks of Oldham County, another kind of family, your inspiration, interest, and support remain constant and deeply appreciated through these sixty-seven years. Special thanks to Sheriff David Medlin, whose initial "tour" through the Middle Alamosa country got me hooked—maps, stories, and all.

And to the landowners, many thanks for trusting me with access to your private wonderlands. Without this, the book could never exist. Especially I thank my ranching neighbors and long-time friends, Tom Henry Green and Lucy McGowan, Bobby Mansfield, and Kim Montgomery. Our daddies would be pleased.

I'm appreciative of the numerous conversations with the staff of the Panhandle-Plains Historical Museum in Canyon, Texas, especially Jeff Indeck, Lisa Jackson, and fellow researcher Alvin Lynn, whose shared insights and information allowed me to grow in my knowledge of geology, archaeology, history, and paleontology.

I'm especially grateful for the unflagging support and warm suggestions of Lex Williford.

And to Beth Hadas, my first book editor those long years ago, for her many astute recommendations throughout this project.

Special thanks to the staff of the Taos Writers Conference. BK Loren, your course spurred rewrites and new vision when I had all but abandoned this project. Demetria Martinez, how much I appreciate your recommendations and encouragement. And Summer Wood, your sage suggestions and generous tips of the trade are greatly appreciated.

To Michael A. Knight and the Helene Wurlitzer Foundation for those blessed summer months and the stimulation of other artists in Taos, where the book found a second life. To Texas Tech University at Junction for the Barry Lopez–led writers' retreat, which gave me the confidence to pursue writing about my own backyard. To the Special Collections staff at Texas Tech University for the resources, assistance, and a Southwest Collection Formby Research Fellowship, which enabled my environmental and historical research. And to the Library at West Texas A&M University, whose collections include essential information on Panhandle history and Kiowa and Comanche peoples. Thank you all.

Many thanks to Harley Shaw, cougar expert extraordinaire. Harley, you are an inspiration and a fount of knowledge always magnanimously shared.

Without conversations with and information graciously given by Christopher Lintz, archaeologist and expert on the Landergin site, I would never have known the salient details of the Antelope Creek people's lives along the Middle Alamosa Creek. I'm grateful, too, for encouragement and information provided by Nita Pahdopony of the Comanche Nation.

I'm appreciative of the University of Texas at El Paso for a sabbatical leave giving me much needed research, writing (and hiking) time for this project.

To my editor, Kathleen Kelly, and her assistant, Bethany Mowry, who provided valuable suggestions with a warmth and seasoned judgment that enhanced this work: you were my other guides. And to all the excellent University of Oklahoma Press staff who made this a better book, especially Patricia Heinicke and Emily Schuster, many thanks.

And of course to you, Deborah Moore. How much I treasure your caring listening and grace while I read passage after passage to you and typed away. As another creative soul, you believed in the meaning of this work and the essential attempt to imaginatively pay homage to those inner and outer home places. Thank you. Thank you.

And finally, to Randy Roark: your passion for the land, your serendipitous poet's heart, your warmth and good nature—as well as your sharing of water, the Ford F150 pickup, and countless afternoons—made this book possible. Without you, I could never have gone "out north." And even if I could have, it wouldn't have been half as meaningful—or half as fun.

3/18